HOW TO PASS

INTERMEDIATE 2
COMPUTING

Frank Frame
John Mason

AN HACHETTE UK COMPANY

Acknowledgements

The Publishers would like to thank the following for permission to reproduce copyright material:

Photo credits
01.04 © Cooperphoto/CORBIS; 01.05 COLIN CUTHBERT/SCIENCE PHOTO LIBRARY; 01.07 © istockphoto; 01.08 © Corbis; 01.09 TEK IMAGE/SCIENCE PHOTO LIBRARY; 01.10 © K-PHOTOS / Alamy; 01.11 © Business Wire via Getty Image; 01.12 © Chris Howes/Wild Places Photography/Alamy; 01.14 Google images © Google Inc. Used with permission; 02.05 Microsoft Windows screen shot(s) reprinted with permission from Microsoft Corporation; 02.06 Microsoft Windows screen shot(s) reprinted with permission from Microsoft Corporation; 03.02 Google images © Google Inc. Used with permission; 03.03 JERRY MASON/SCIENCE PHOTO LIBRARY; 03.04 Microsoft Hotmail screen shot(s) reprinted with permission from Microsoft Corporation; 03.05 Google images © Google Inc. Used with permission; 04.03 © 2002 Oddcast, Inc. All rights reserved; 04.07 © Geoff du Feu/Alamy; 04.09 MAXIMILIAN STOCK LTD/SCIENCE PHOTO LIBRARY; 04.10 © Yiorgos Karahalis/Reuters/Corbis; 05.01 Microsoft FrontPage screen shot(s) reprinted with permission from Microsoft Corporation; 05.02 Logo courtesy of the Mozilla Foundation; 05.03 © James Leynse/Corbis; 05.04 Screenshot is © 2007 Corel Corporation, reprinted by permission; 05.05 © Julian Hawkins/Rex; 05.06 Reproduced by kind permission of Steinberg Media Technologies GmbH; 05.07 © isifa Image Service s.r.o./Alamy; 05.08 © istockphoto; 05.11 Reproduced by kind permission of Steinberg Media Technologies GmbH; 05.12 Microsoft Audacity screen shot(s) reprinted with permission from Microsoft Corporation; 05.14 Reproduced by kind permission of Steinberg Media Technologies GmbH; 05.15 Reproduced by kind permission of Steinberg Media Technologies GmbH; 05.16 Reproduced by kind permission of Steinberg Media Technologies GmbH; 05.17 © istockphoto; 05.19 Microsoft Windows Moviemaker screen shot(s) reprinted with permission from Microsoft Corporation; 05.20 Microsoft Windows Moviemaker screen shot(s) reprinted with permission from Microsoft Corporation.

Index compiled by Indexing Specialists (UK) Ltd.

Every effort has been made to trace all copyright holders, but if any have been inadvertently overlooked the Publishers will be pleased to make the necessary arrangements at the first opportunity.

Although every effort has been made to ensure that website addresses are correct at time of going to press, Hodder Gibson cannot be held responsible for the content of any website mentioned in this book. It is sometimes possible to find a relocated web page by typing in the address of the home page for a website in the URL window of your browser.

Hachette's policy is to use papers that are natural, renewable and recyclable products and made from wood grown in sustainable forests. The logging and manufacturing processes are expected to conform to the environmental regulations of the country of origin.

Orders: please contact Bookpoint Ltd, 130 Milton Park, Abingdon, Oxon OX14 4SB. Telephone: (44) 01235 827720. Fax: (44) 01235 400454. Lines are open 9.00–5.00, Monday to Saturday, with a 24-hour message answering service. Visit our website at www.hoddereducation.co.uk. Hodder Gibson can be contacted direct on:
Tel: 0141 848 1609; Fax: 0141 889 6315; email: hoddergibson@hodder.co.uk

Dedication
To Ruth and Michael – Thanks for all the joy you bring me.
John Mason

© Frank Frame, John Mason 2008, 2009
First published in 2008 by
Hodder Gibson, an imprint of Hodder Education,
An Hachette UK company,
2a Christie Street
Paisley PA1 1NB

This colour edition first published 2009

Impression number   5 4 3 2 1
Year   2012 2011 2010 2009

All rights reserved. Apart from any use permitted under UK copyright law, no part of this publication may be reproduced or transmitted in any form or by any means, electronic or mechanical, including photocopying and recording, or held within any information storage and retrieval system, without permission in writing from the publisher or under licence from the Copyright Licensing Agency Limited. Further details of such licences (for reprographic reproduction) may be obtained from the Copyright Licensing Agency Limited, Saffron House, 6–10 Kirby Street, London EC1N 8TS.

Cover photo © PHOTOTAKE Inc./Alamy
Typeset in 10.5 on 14pt Frutiger Light by Phoenix Photosetting, Chatham, Kent
Printed in Italy

A catalogue record for this title is available from the British Library

ISBN-13: 978 1444 108 361

CONTENTS

Introduction 1

Chapter 1   Computer Systems 2

Chapter 2   Software Development 29

Chapter 3   Computer Networking 48

Chapter 4   Artificial Intelligence 60

Chapter 5   Multimedia Technology 80

Chapter 6   Focus on the External Examination 101

Answers 107

Index 117

INTRODUCTION

This book is designed to help you pass Intermediate 2 Computing. The book covers all units in the course: the two core units – Computer Systems and Software Development – as well as all three optional units – Computer Networking, Multimedia Technology and Artificial Intelligence.

The material covers all the topics in the content grids in the SQA Intermediate 2 Computing arrangements document. It also contains sets of questions covering the content of each topic.

Finally, there is also a chapter focusing on the external exam. This contains information on the exam, tips on exam preparation and a set of exam style questions.

How to use this book

Use the book to check up on your knowledge of each of the core topics and your optional topic. Attempt all the questions. The answers are at the back of the book. Attempt all the problem-solving questions and check the answers. Read the tips about exam preparation and come up with your own revision plan! Finally, attempt the exam style questions and check the answers.

If you do all this you will greatly improve your chances of passing Intermediate 2 Computing.

Chapter 1

COMPUTER SYSTEMS

Data representation – representing numbers, text and graphics

Using binary to represent positive numbers

We use the decimal numbers 0, 1, 2, 3, 4, 5, 6, 7, 8, 9.

Computers use binary numbers. To work with decimals, the computer has to convert them. The table below will help you understand how to convert them.

2^7	2^6	2^5	2^4	2^3	2^2	2^1	2^0	Power of 2
128	64	32	16	8	4	2	1	Decimal equivalent

The decimal number 66 is stored as **01000010** in binary.

2^7	2^6	2^5	2^4	2^3	2^2	2^1	2^0	Power of 2
128	64	32	16	8	4	2	1	Decimal
0	1	0	0	0	0	1	0	= 64 + 2 = 66

Advantages of using binary numbers
1. Binary is a simple two-state system (1 or 0) which is ideal when representing a two-state system of 'power on/power off'.
2. There are only a few rules for addition, making calculations simpler.

Floating point representation of real numbers

In floating point notation, numbers are divided into base/mantissa/exponent.

Any number which is a power of 10 can be represented with a decimal point in a fixed position and so $192.507 = .192507*10^3$

Mantissa	Exponent	Base
.192507	3	10

Using this system $18.3506 = .183506*10^2$
$183,506 = .183506*10^6$
$18,350,600 = .183506*10^8$

The performance of a computer is sometimes measured in terms of how many millions of floating point operations per second it can perform.

Advantages of using floating point
Floating point is easy to implement and saves storage space.

Chapter 1

 ## Measuring the size of memory

We use these terms to measure a computer's memory:

1 bit   Binary digit: a single 1 or 0
1 byte   = 8 bits e.g. 11001110
1 kilobyte   = 1024 bytes
1 megabyte = 1024 kilobytes
1 gigabyte   = 1024 megabytes
1 terabyte   = 1024 gigabytes

Questions

Q1   What is the binary number for 47, 80, 34?

Q2   State two advantages of floating point.

Q3   How many megabytes of data can be stored on a 120 gigabyte hard disk?

Key Points

Representing text

Character set
The character set is the group of letters and numbers and characters that the computer can represent and manipulate.

ASCII
Text is represented using **ASCII** code.

ASCII stands for **A**merican **S**tandard **C**ode for **I**nformation **I**nterchange.

Each character in the character set has a unique value. All characters are included:

- non-printing characters e.g. <return>, <tab>, <escape>
- upper and lower case letters e.g. A–Z, a–z
- numbers e.g. 0–9
- punctuation and other symbols e.g. $ & * ^ @ " :

An extract of the binary code is shown below:

Binary	Decimal	Representing
01000001	65	A
01000010	66	B
01000011	67	C
01000100	68	D
01000101	69	E
01000110	70	F

Key Points continued

COMPUTER SYSTEMS

Chapter 1

Key Points continued

Control characters

Control characters are the first 32 characters of the ASCII set. They each have a control function, for example:

Binary	Decimal	Representing
00000001	1	Start of header
00000010	2	Start of text
00000011	3	End of text
00000100	4	End of transmission

These are often used when transmitting data and include keys such as <return>, <tab> and <delete>.

Key Points

Representing black and white graphics

Graphics (drawings, graphs or pictures) are made up of **pixels**, points on the screen. Look at Figure 1.1.

Pixels are represented by patterns of binary numbers where each square or pixel filled in = 1, each square or pixel left blank = 0.

Calculating the storage space for black and white graphics

Look at the graphic shown and follow these steps:

Figure 1.1

- Calculate the number of pixels needed, in this case 8 × 8 = 64 pixels.
- Each pixel in black and white requires 1 bit to store it, which equals 64 bits.
- Divide by 8 for bytes, 64/8 = 8 bytes.
- If the answer is more than 1024 continue to divide by 1024 for KB, MB, etc.

Graphics tend to be much larger than this simple example.

Key Points continued ➢

Chapter 1

Key Points continued

Example

Calculate the size of a graphic which is 6 inches by 6 inches at 300 pixels per inch.

- 1800 × 1800 pixels = 3240000 pixels.
- For a black and white graphic this requires 3240000 bits.
- 3240000/8 = 405000 bytes.
- 405000/1024 = **395.5 kilobytes**.

Questions

Q4 What is ASCII code used to represent?

Q5 How are control characters different from the rest of the ASCII code?

Q6 Calculate the storage requirements for a black and white graphic 4 inches by 5 inches at 600 pixels per inch.

Computer structure

Figure 1.2 is a simple diagram of a computer system.

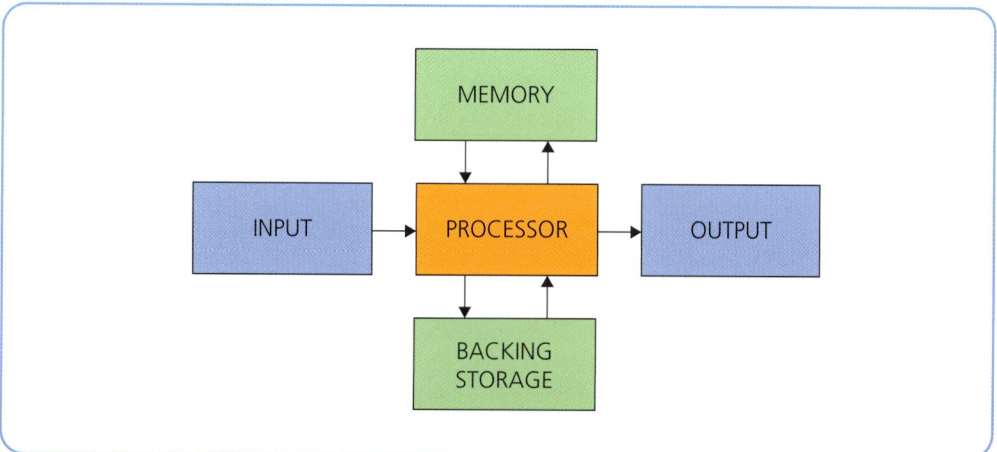

Figure 1.2

As you can see the processor is at the centre of the system.

Chapter 1

What You Should Know

About the processor

The purpose of a processor

The processor, also called the microprocessor or chip, is the 'brains' of the computer that deals with all the movement of data and any calculations to be carried out.

The Processor is made up of three important components:

- the Control Unit – CU
- the Arithmetic and Logic Unit – ALU
- registers.

The **Control Unit** sends control signals to:

- store data in memory
- fetch data from memory
- decode and carry out instructions.

The **Arithmetic and Logic Unit** carries out all the computer's **arithmetic** and **logical** functions:

- arithmetic functions such as addition, subtraction, multiplication
- logic functions such as comparing values using IF, AND, OR, >, <, equals.

Registers are small *temporary* memory locations located *on* **the processor**. They are used to store data, instructions and memory addresses.

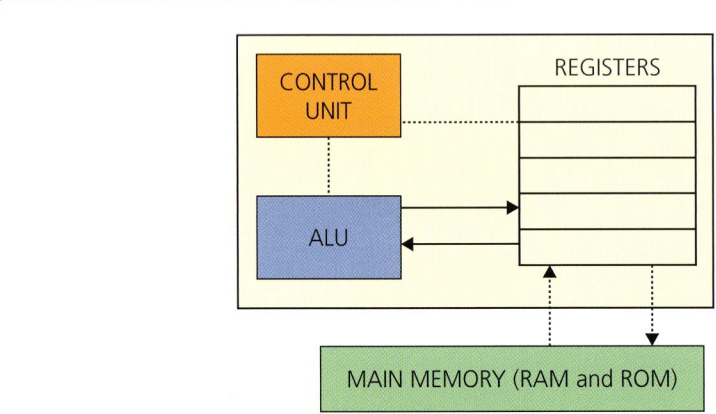

Figure 1.3 A computer processor

Chapter 1

COMPUTER SYSTEMS

What You Should Know

About backing storage and main memory

Backing storage

All storage devices outside of the main processor, e.g. hard drives, CD drives, USB flash memory, are known as backing storage.

Main memory

Main memory is located inside the computer system.

Main memory can be either **RAM** or **ROM**.

RAM: Random Access Memory

- The processor can write to, or read from, RAM at high speed.
- Data held in RAM can be changed.
- All data in RAM is **lost** when the power is switched off.
- RAM is the working space of the computer. It holds all of the programs and data files currently in use.

ROM: Read Only Memory

- Data is stored permanently in ROM, it is **not lost** when the power goes off.
- Data in the ROM cannot be changed.
- ROM holds vital systems data and programs.

What You Should Know

About embedded systems

These are small-scale computer systems, complete with their own processors and memory, built into machines to enable them to carry out their functions. Many embedded systems have a simple control panel or touch screen to enable the user to select functions.

You find embedded systems in a wide range of products and machinery such as digital cameras, mobile phones, microwaves, washing machines, cars, printers.

Types of computer system

Palmtop computer

A palmtop computer is a small computer designed to fit in your hand or pocket.

Palmtops are used for storing and retrieving data, keeping a diary of appointments, as an MP3 player, communicating with a network and a host of other uses. Palmtops are merging with mobile phones to produce 'smartphones'.

Chapter 1

A palmtop:
- is smaller than a laptop (it fits onto your hand)
- is very light, weighing less than 200 g
- has a small, on-screen, keyboard
- has a touch sensitive screen
- has a full range of GPPs, although they are cut-down versions
- allows the user to input using a pen (or *stylus*)
- is powered by a small battery
- stores data on a *flashcard*.

Laptop computer

A laptop:
- is small enough to use on your lap comfortably
- is useful for working away from the home or office
- takes up little space and can be carried easily
- is light, weighing less than 4 kg
- is powered by batteries (or by mains adaptor)
- has an LCD (Liquid Crystal Display) or TFT (Thin Film Transistor) screen
- has a standard keyboard as well as a range of disk drives.

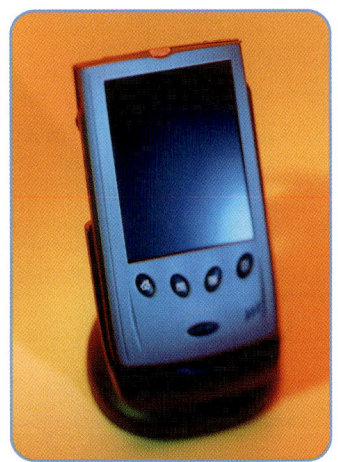

Figure 1.4 A palmtop

Desktop computer

A desktop:
- is made up of a monitor, a keyboard, mouse, processor, main memory and the hard disk drive, CD and DVD drives
- is reasonably compact and will fit onto a workstation or desk.

Mainframe computer

A mainframe:
- is a very large computer
- has powerful processors, with a large internal memory capacity and large-capacity backing storage measured in terabytes
- can work at high speeds, accessing and storing data as well as processing transactions
- often has many terminals connected to the processor which allows many people to use the system at the same time – this is called multi-access.

Multi-access computers are so powerful and fast that people are not aware that they are sharing the system with lots of others.

Banks, mail order companies, universities and other large organisations use mainframes.

Figure 1.5 A mainframe computer

Chapter 1

What You Should Know

About clock speed
- The clock pulses regulate and co-ordinate the activities in the processor.
- These pulses are measured in megahertz (MHz) or gigahertz (GHz).
- 1 MHz = 1 million pulses per second, 1 GHz = 1000 MHz second.
- Clock speed is one simple measure of the power of a processor.
- Processor clock speeds are changing all the time.

How good a measure of performance is it?
The clock speed does give you an indication of the performance of the processor which is at the heart of system, but you must be careful not to over-emphasise its importance.

The performance of a processor is not dictated by the speed of the clock alone, though this is one of the headline factors that adverts and salespeople will emphasise.

Questions

Q7 What is the purpose of a processor?

Q8 What is the job of the ALU?

Q9 What is a register?

Q10 What is the key difference between backing storage and main memory?

Q11 What happens to the data held in RAM and ROM when the system is switched off?

Q12 What is an embedded system?

Q13 Describe two differences between:

(a) a laptop and a desktop

(b) a desktop and a mainframe.

Q14 What is a processor's clock speed measured in?

Q15 Check the Internet to get the clock speed of the latest processors.

Chapter 1

What You Should Know

About input devices

Keyboard

Keyboards are useful input devices and are used for typing in data and commands.

Mouse

A mouse lets the user interact with the computer system. The hand-sized case of the mouse has at least one button on top and a ball or laser fitted underneath. Sensors detect the movement of the mouse and whether a button has been pressed. The mouse is used to control the cursor on the screen and to manipulate icons and menus.

Figure 1.6

Microphone

A microphone is used to input sound data.

Touchpad/trackpad

A touchpad is a small pad, usually found on laptops, with sensors that detect the movements and taps of your finger. This lets the user control the position of the pointer on the screen and select icons and open menus. Touchpads are more convenient when using a laptop on the move in places where it is difficult to use a mouse.

Digital camera

A digital camera is a camera for taking digital pictures. The quality is measured in megapixels: the number of millions of detectors in the grid that detect the picture. A reasonably good digital camera will be 8 megapixels and will cost less than £200. Advantages: they can hold lots of images without film; you can delete the pictures you don't want; you can transfer pictures to a computer and print them out.

Scanner

A scanner enables the user to capture images, like photos or documents, onto the computer in a digital form.

Figure 1.7 A digital camera

The scanner shines a light on the document and reads in the reflected light. It then changes this data into binary and sends it to the computer.

Webcam

Webcams are digital cameras which are used to take still photos or capture moving images.

In some cases the images are then transferred to a web page and then sent across the Internet and are used for such things as viewing traffic flowing along motorways, for advertising tourist attractions and/or business sites. They can also be used to set up video conferencing.

Chapter 1

COMPUTER SYSTEMS

Comparing input devices

Comparison criteria	What it means	Example
Resolution	This determines the quality of images that are captured e.g. by digital cameras.	An 8 megapixel digital camera. A 900 dpi printer.
Capacity	The amount of data that can be stored on the input device: usually measured in megabytes and gigabytes.	A digital camera with a 1 gigabyte memory card.
Speed of data transfer	The speed at which the data is transferred to the computer: usually measured in kilobits per second (kbps).	This can be difficult with input devices as the transfer speeds are not easily available.
Cost	What you have to pay!	This varies all the time.

Practical Task:
Use the Internet to get the latest information on input devices: check, where appropriate, for resolution, capacity, speed of transfer and cost.

Questions

Q16 Copy and complete the table, stating which input device you would use to:

Input a graphic from a book
Control a pointer on a laptop
Capture and send pictures across the Internet
Capture sound

Q17 Name two characteristics you could use to compare two digital cameras.

What You Should Know

About output devices

Monitor
The screen used to display computer output is called a monitor. Different monitors have different resolutions and different quality levels. The higher the resolution the clearer the image.

What you should know continued ➤

Chapter 1

What You Should Know continued

High resolution monitors are needed for CAD (computer aided design) work and art work.

There are three types of monitor: CRT (chunky ones like the image on the left), LCD (Liquid Crystal Display) and TFT (Thin Film Transistor). The last two are flat screens.

Figure 1.8 A CRT monitor

Liquid Crystal Display (LCD)

LCD screens use transistors and a thin film of liquid crystals to control the light passing through the screen. They are often found on palmtop and laptop computers because they are light, compact and need little power and can be run on batteries. One problem is that some LCD screens are not very bright and can cause eye strain if they are used for too long.

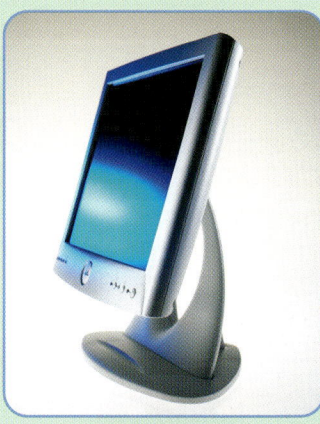

Thin Film Transistor (TFT)

Figure 1.9 An LCD monitor

TFT is a type of LCD screen that uses lots of transistors to produce a high quality display. A TFT screen can display animations and 3-D graphics much more clearly than ordinary LCD screens. The disadvantage is that they can be a lot more expensive than ordinary LCD screens.

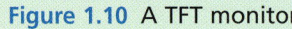

Figure 1.10 A TFT monitor

Comparing monitors

Comparison criteria	What it means	Example
Resolution	This determines the quality of images that can be displayed.	A 1680 × 1050 high resolution screen or a 1280 × 1024 medium resolution.
Cost	What you have to pay!	This varies all the time.

What you should know continued ➤

Chapter 1

What You Should Know continued

Practical Task:
Use the Internet to get the latest information on output devices. Check, where appropriate, for resolution and cost.

Inkjet printer

This printer sprays ink onto paper to form letters and pictures. It produces high quality output and is less expensive to buy than a laser printer. However, running costs can be high as the toner is expensive (and it dries out if you don't use it often). Inkjet printers are also a lot slower than laser printers.

Laser printer

This works by using a laser beam to put the image of a page onto a photosensitive drum. The toner or ink then sticks to the charged drum. This is then transferred to paper and fused by heat to make it stick. Laser printers are very fast and produce very high quality output. However, they can be more expensive to buy than an inkjet.

Comparing printers

Comparison criteria	What it means
Speed	This is measured in pages per minute (ppm) e.g. 8 ppm.
Resolution	The higher the resolution, the more dots per inch (dpi), the better the quality of the printout. Printouts from a printer capable of 900 dpi will be poorer in quality than those from a 1200 dpi printer.
Cost	Capital cost: the initial cost of buying the printer. Running costs: cost of toner or ink (and paper).

Practical Task:
Use the Internet to get the latest information on printers. Check for speed, resolution and cost.

Loudspeakers

Loudspeakers enable your computer to output music, multimedia presentations with voice-overs and sound effects, videos and even discussions on a video conference link. Most PCs come with a small set of speakers fitted, but you can splash out and buy a set of speakers like those shown to give you that full surround sound.

Figure 1.11 Loudspeakers

COMPUTER SYSTEMS

Chapter 1

Questions

Q18 Check out the Internet to find an example of a colour laser printer; write down the speed, resolution and cost.

Q19 Check out the Internet to find an example of:

(a) a TFT high resolution screen;

(b) a medium resolution CRT monitor.

Backing storage devices

This category covers all storage devices outside of the main processor.

Below is a table of backing storage devices.

Magnetic	Optical	Solid state
Floppy disks	CD-ROM	USB Flash Drive
Hard disks	CD-R	
Zip disks	CD-RW	
Magnetic tapes	DVD-ROM	
	DVD-R	
	DVD-RW	

What You Should Know

About magnetic storage

Floppy disk

Floppy disks are cheap magnetic storage devices with a limited storage capacity. High density disks hold 1.44 megabytes of data.

Advantages	Disadvantages
Small in size and easy to handle. Cheap per disk. Portable.	Damaged easily by heat, dust, dampness, electromagnetic fields. Small capacity.

What you should know continued ➢

Chapter 1

What You Should Know continued

Hard disk

A metal disk with magnetised surfaces on which data is stored as patterns of magnetic spots. The disks are in sealed units to stop dust and dirt corrupting data. They are usually fixed in the computer, but you can get portable external drives.

Advantages	Disadvantages
Fast access times, direct access. Fast data transfer rates. Cheap per megabyte.	Not usually portable. Can be damaged if dropped.

Figure 1.12

Tape

Plastic tapes, like audio or video tapes, that store data in binary using magnetic 'spots' to encode the data. Tapes are often used for making backups and use sequential access to data.

What You Should Know

About optical storage

CD-ROM

This stands for 'Compact Disk – Read Only Memory'. It is an example of optical storage. It is fast and can store up to 700 MB of data. It cannot be written to, the data is fixed at time of manufacture. The data is read by a sensor that detects laser light reflected from the surface of the disk.

The speed of a CD drive is given as a number e.g. 52X (meaning 52 times 150 kbps).

CD-R

This is CD-recordable; it allows you to record data **once**. Once data is recorded on it, it works just like a CD-ROM. It is read only. It can hold 700 MB. The speed of a CD-R drive is given as two numbers, the **read** speed and the **write** speed.

CD-RW

This is a CD-rewriteable on which you can record data over and over again, just like hard disks. You can use them to make backups of large files, e.g. groups of photos, and you can change the data stored on the disk as often as you want. A CD-RW has three speeds: one for **writing** data, one for **re-writing** and one for **reading**. For example write 52X, re-write 24X and read 52X.

What you should know continued ➤

COMPUTER SYSTEMS

15

Chapter 1

What You Should Know continued

DVD-ROM

A DVD-ROM uses optical technology to read data. Like a CD-ROM it is read only. A DVD-ROM has much larger capacity data than a CD-ROM. Single-sided single-layered DVDs have a capacity of 4.7 gigabytes. Double-sided multi-layered DVDs have a capacity of 17 gigabytes. The speed of a DVD-ROM drive is given as a number, e.g. 16X. This is different from a CD, as each 1X is 1250 kilobits per second (kbps), so 16X is 16 × 1250 kbps.

DVD-R

DVD-recordable allows you to record data once. After recording, the data cannot be changed. They have the same capacity as DVDs but have two speeds, one for **writing** and one for **reading** data, e.g. write 6X, read 12X.

DVD-RW

This is a DVD that allows you to record data over and over again. Like hard disks, you can use them to make backups of very large files, e.g. home movies from your digital video camera, and you can change the data stored on the disk as often as you want.

A DVD-RW has three speeds, one for **writing** data, one for **re-writing** and one for **reading**, e.g. write 6X, re-write 2.4X and read 12X.

What You Should Know

About solid state storage

USB flash drive

A re-writable memory chip that holds its data when it is removed from the computer. It is a handy portable form of backing storage that fits into your pocket.

What You Should Know

About types of data access

The two types of data access you have to know about are **sequential** access and **random** access, also called **direct** access.

Sequential access is used for magnetic tape. It means that when you want a specific piece of data that is halfway through the tape, you have to wind all the way through before you can read it.

In **random/direct access** there is no wait time while the disk scans through earlier data; the read head goes straight to the address where the data is held.

To give an example, if you were trying to play track five of your favourite album on CD you would jump straight to the track and play it. If the album is on tape, you would have to wait while the tape drive fast-forwarded to the start of track five.

Chapter 1

Practical Task:
You need to be able to compare backing storage devices according to their **capacity**, **speed of data transfer** and **cost**. Copy and complete a table like the one below using the latest information from magazines and the Internet.

Type of backing storage	Name and model	Capacity	Speed of data transfer	Cost per megabyte	Type of access
Tape drive					
Floppy disk					
Hard disk					
USB flash drive					
CD-ROM					
CD-R					
CD-RW					
DVD-ROM					
DVD-RW					

Interfaces

Interfaces are needed between the processor and peripherals.

Computer peripherals such as CD-ROM drives, scanners, keyboards all have different characteristics:

- They have different data transfer rates.
- They use a wide variety of codes and control signals.
- Some transmit data in serial form and others in parallel form.
- Some, such as keyboards, even work at higher voltages than the processor.
- They all operate at much slower speeds than the processor.

Key Points

Interfaces

The interface is the combination of hardware and software needed to link the processor to the peripherals and to enable them to communicate with the processor despite all their differing characteristics.

What does the interface do?

An interface will do jobs like:
- change electrical voltages
- deal with control signals
- change analogue data to digital form
- store incoming data so that the processor can get on with other tasks.

COMPUTER SYSTEMS

17

Chapter 1

Questions

Q20 Describe the difference in capacity between a CD-ROM and a DVD-ROM.

Q21 What is a USB flash drive used for?

Q22 What type of backing storage uses sequential access?

Q23 (a) Why is an interface needed?
(b) Name two jobs an interface does.

Networking

These tables will help you compare the different types of computer networks.

	Local area network (LAN)
Functions	Sharing of data files, of peripherals, enabling communication via email.
Geographical spread	Limited to one building such as a school, an office block or a factory. The limit is usually up to two kilometres.
Transmission media	Twisted pair copper cable, fibre-optic cable, co-axial cable.
Bandwidth	The bandwidth available depends on the transmission media: ◆ twisted pair copper cable: 10–100 Mbits per second; ◆ fibre-optic cable; ◆ co-axial cable.

	Wide area network (WAN)
Functions	Supports transfer of files, communication via email, shared use of multi-user databases, conferencing.
Geographical spread	There is no physical limitation to a WAN. It could cover a city, a country or stretch around the world.
Transmission media	Telecommunication systems covering large distances.
Bandwidth	The bandwidth available depends on the nature of the telecommunications link. If you are connected to a WAN using a dialup modem you are limited to 56 Kbits per second. An ISDN line could support up to 128 Kbits per second and using a leased telecoms T3 line would support a 44.7 megabits per second transmission.

Chapter 1

COMPUTER SYSTEMS

Internetwork	
Functions	An internetwork consists of several networks joined by devices such as routers or switches. The functions available to the users are those available on LANs; see table on previous page.
Geographical spread	An internetwork can vary in its geographical spread. It could be used to link several LANs in the same complex or, using the telecom system, it could link networks spread across a city or a country.
Transmission media	This depends on the configuration of the Internetwork. If it is linking several LANs in the same geographical location it would probably use a high speed backbone medium such as fibre-optic cable. If it is linking over a wide geographical area it would use a form of broadband connection over the telecommunication system.
Bandwidth	Using a fibre-optic cable to link LANs would support a bandwidth of up to 100 gigabits per second. Linking networks across a wide area would involve using telecommunications such as those used by a WAN. Using a DSL broadband connection, a domestic user can have a bandwidth of 10 megabits per second and upwards.

Key Points

The advantages of networks

The advantages of networks are that users can:
- share peripherals such as hard drives and printers
- share data and programs
- work on shared projects
- communicate by sending emails
- backup data more effectively
- control security more effectively.

What You Should Know

About email

Reading your email

In order to read your email you have to enter your own ID and password.

What you should know continued ➢

Chapter 1

What You Should Know continued

Sending an email

To send an email you need to enter an email address, for example, joesoap@yahoo.co.uk.

'joesoap' is the ID of the person you are sending the email to and '@yahoo.co.uk' is the server which processes his mail.

Replying to an email

Email software has a reply button that enables you to reply without having to type in the email address again.

Setting up an address book

If you send emails regularly to the same people, it is a good idea to store their email addresses in an electronic address book.

Setting up mailing lists

If the messages that are sent need to go to several people at the same time, use mailing lists, sometimes called distribution lists, which contain all the email addresses of the people in the group.

Setting up folders

To organise your emails, you can set up a hierarchy of folders and set up rules to have the email messages delivered directly to the correct folder.

Key Points

The World Wide Web

Web pages

The graphical part of the Internet, the **World Wide Web**, carries most of the traffic on the Internet. It is made up of multimedia web pages that are stored on computers across the world. Web pages hold text, sounds, graphics, animations, and videos. These are linked together by **hyperlinks.**

Hyperlinks

A hyperlink appears either as underlined text or as a graphic, like the one shown here. Clicking on a hyperlink instructs the browser to fetch a web page and display it.

Figure 1.13 A hyperlink graphic

Key Points continued ➢

Chapter 1

Key Points continued

Browser

A browser is a program that helps you navigate the world wide web, move between and look at web pages. You can enter the address of the page you want to go to or you can click on a hyperlink.

Search engines

Search engines are used to look for web pages. A **simple search** has one item or topic in the search, e.g. 'Computer Network LAN'.

The search engine will find all the web pages related to that topic and send the results to your computer for your browser to display them. You must be careful how you word searches as the search engine often only looks for the words and not the phrase. For example, the above search would display the pages with the whole phrase, but also any page with one or more of the words in them. There are a lot of pages on the Internet with the word 'computer' in them!

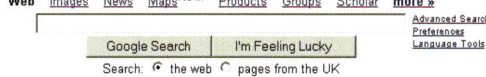

Figure 1.14 A search engine

Key Points

Why are computer networks so popular?

The cost of telecommunication services is getting cheaper all the time
There are so many companies competing to connect homes and businesses to the Internet that the cost of broadband connections keeps falling.

Sharing expensive equipment
Network users can share equipment like backing storage, cameras and printers.

Businesses and families are spread around the world
Networks let businesses and families keep in touch around the world.

Key Points continued ➣

21

Chapter 1

Key Points continued

We all need up-to-date information
- Students need it for their education.
- Businesses need it to work efficiently.
- People need it to buy, sell and book holidays.

Questions

Q24 Copy and complete this table.

Telecommunications are used on a:	
The media used on a LAN are:	
The maximum spread of a LAN is:	
The bandwidth on a LAN using copper cable can be:	

Q25 State two advantages of using a network.

Q26 What is (a) a mailing list; (b) a browser; (c) a hyperlink; (d) a search engine?

Q27 Give four reasons why networks are so popular.

Computers and the law

Key Points

The Data Protection Act

There is a need to protect people's privacy regarding information held about them on computer systems. People have right of access to data that is held about them on computer systems. There are exceptions to this right. For example, you have no right of access if the data is held by the Police, security forces or the Inland Revenue.

There are three groups of people named in the Act. These are **data subjects**, **data users** and **data controllers**.

Key Points continued >

Chapter 1

COMPUTER SYSTEMS

Key Points continued

Data subjects

In the Act individuals to whom data relates are known as **data subjects**. Data subjects have the following rights:

- To know if data is held about them on a computer system and to have a copy and a description of that data.
- To know the purposes for which the data is being processed and who is going to receive the data.
- To inspect such data and to have it changed if they think it is shown to be inaccurate.
- To ask for compensation if data is inaccurate or if an unauthorised person has been given access to it.
- To prevent processing of data likely to cause damage or distress.
- To be sure that decisions made about them are not made only on the basis of automatic processing, e.g. psychometric testing for jobs.

For each of these a data subject can be charged a single administration fee. A data subject can apply to the courts to block the processing of data or to correct, erase or destroy it.

Data user

A **data user** is an individual within an organisation who makes use of personal data.

The data user must keep to the following **data protection principles**.

All personal data should be:

- processed only if the consent of the individual is given, if it is part of a legal contract, if it is essential to a business transaction or to the carrying out of public duties
- held for the specified purposes described in the **Register** entry
- accurate and where necessary kept up to date
- relevant and not excessive in relation to the purpose for which it is held
- adequate for the purpose specified
- processed in accordance with the rights of the data subject
- surrounded by proper security, like passwords and/or encryption
- transferred only to countries outside of the EU that have adequate security measures as defined in the Act.

Data controller

The **data controller** is defined as the person, business or organisation who controls the collection and use of personal data.

The data controller must:

- register with the **Information Commissioner**
- apply for permission to keep personal data on computers
- state what data they want to keep, its purpose and who has access to it.

Key Points continued

23

Chapter 1

Key Points continued

Register of Data Controllers
Details about who holds information on members of the public on computer systems is held in the Register of Data Controllers, which is to be found in central libraries.

Information Commissioner
If anyone has a problem accessing data or has a complaint about the accuracy of data, they can contact the office of the Information Commissioner, who oversees the administration of the Act.

Exceptions to the Act
If the data is held by the Police, the security forces or the Inland Revenue then access is denied.

Key Points

Copyright Designs and Patents Act
This deals with the problem of computer software, which is now protected by law for 50 years after it is published. It is illegal to:

- make unauthorised (pirate) copies of software
- run pirate software
- transmit software over telecommunications links and copy it
- run multiple copies of software if only one copy was purchased
- give, lend or sell copies of bought software unless license to do so is granted.

Key Points

The Computer Misuse Act
This act is designed to make hacking into a computer system illegal and subject to penalties. This act makes it an offence to gain unauthorised access to a computer system or to make unauthorised modifications to computer materials.

The Act specifies modifying computer material as:

- interfering with a system so that it doesn't run properly
- making changes to the system to prevent others accessing the system
- making changes to the software or data.

Penalties of up to five years imprisonment and fines apply.

Chapter 1

Questions

Q28 Describe each of the following: data subject, data controller, data user.

Q29 List three principles of the Data Protection Act which a user must keep to.

Q30 What is 'modifying computer materials' defined as in the Computer Misuse Act?

Q31 List three activities made illegal by the Copyright Designs and Patents Act.

Computer software

Definition of an operating system

An operating system (OS) is a program, or set of programs, that controls all the tasks your computer carries out. Without the operating system no other tasks could take place. It runs other software, controls peripherals, monitors the operation of the computer and provides the human–computer interface (HCI) for the user.

There are many different operating systems available today, but three of the most common are Microsoft Windows XP, LINUX and Apple OS X.

Application program

An application program is a program designed to let the computer user carry out tasks, for example, spreadsheet, word processing, graphics applications.

Key Points

File formats

Text documents can be saved in different file formats. The most common are ASCII, Text, and RTF.

Advantage of using a standard format

When you save a text document using a standard file format you can be sure that the files will be accepted by a wide range of software. The result is that your data files are very portable and can be transferred easily from one package to another.

ASCII

An ASCII file stores information about the characters in a document. It does not store information about the styles, the fonts, the spacing, simply the bare text. It is such a simple file format it is accepted by virtually all computer systems. So ASCII files are very portable. Also, because they don't contain additional information they are smaller than the equivalent rich text file. This means they wont take up as much space on your hard disk and will take less time to transmit across a network.

Key Points continued ➤

25

COMPUTER SYSTEMS

Chapter 1

Key Points continued

Text
This format is virtually identical to ASCII. It encodes plain text with no formatting information. There is a text format which includes the <return> code which allows it to divide text into paragraphs. Files saved in text format, like ASCII files, are relatively small, take up less space on backing storage and take less time to transmit.

Rich text format (RTF)
Rich text format files store the information about the text and the information about paragraphing, indentation, styles, fonts and sizes.

What You Should Know

About objects and operations
You need to be able to identify the main data objects that can be found in word processing, databases, spreadsheets and graphic packages and also be able to state the actions or operations that can be carried out on them. The table below should help you.

Package	Object	Operations
Word processor	Character Word Sentence Paragraph Page Table	Enter, insert, edit, delete, copy, paste, format, spellcheck, search and replace. Add row, add column. Split cell, merge cell.
Database	Field Record File Layout	Enter, insert, edit, delete, copy, paste, format, search, sort, calculate.
Spreadsheet	Cell Row Column Number Text Formula Chart	Enter, insert, edit, delete, copy, paste, set attributes, format, calculate (sum, average, max, min, if), chart.
Graphics	Line Circle Rectangle Polygon	Enter, insert, edit, delete, copy, paste, format, scale, rotate, crop, group, ungroup, layer.

Chapter 1

COMPUTER SYSTEMS

Key Points

Virus

What is a virus?
A virus is a destructive piece of software that attaches itself to a file, reproduces itself, and spreads to other files.

A virus will often lurk in a system before disrupting it, for example, by corrupting data.

How does a virus operate?
Viruses attach themselves to applications, games, system files and even data files such as word-processing documents or graphics.

Signs of a virus
If your computer has a virus it might do one or more of the following:
- display odd messages
- receive lots of junk mail
- lose or corrupt files
- make weird sounds or display odd graphics
- restart when you don't want it to.

What You Should Know

About how viruses are spread
Viruses are spread by:
- people swapping or lending CDs
- email attachments. Viruses can use your email address book to spread themselves.

Anti-virus software stops viruses spreading
Make sure your computer has anti-virus software loaded, running and regularly updated!

27

Chapter 1

Questions

Q32 List three jobs performed by an operating system.

Q33 Why is an operating system so important?

Q34 Give three examples of an application package.

Q35 What is the advantage of using standard file formats?

Q36 How is a file saved as RTF different from the same file saved in ASCII format?

Q37 How does a virus operate?

Q38 How are viruses spread?

Chapter 2

SOFTWARE DEVELOPMENT

When you are first given a problem to solve using a computer the first thing you do is think 'What is it I have just been asked to do?' The last thing you do is ask the question 'Does what I have written actually solve the problem?' All the stuff in between is what **Software Development** is all about.

The Software Development unit covers four areas:
- the software development process
- software development languages and environments
- high level programming language constructs
- standard algorithms.

The software development process

The seven stages of the software development process are **analysis**, **design**, **implementation**, **testing**, **documentation**, **evaluation** and **maintenance**. If you have done any formal programming at all it is likely you will have completed the first six in some form.

You have to be able to name the seven stages **in order** and to give a brief description of what happens at each stage. If you don't have a good memory, try to think of a sentence where the first letters of each word follow the same pattern as the stages **ADITDEM**. You could try 'All Dogs In The Dairy Eat Meat', or a phrase like 'A Dire IT DEMo'. Maybe the word ADITDEM sounds like a bit of Morse Code – 'A DIT DEM'. Whatever works for you!

Analysis stage

Analysis is what happens when you are first given the task and have to work out what you actually have to do. It is when the boundaries of the problem are formally agreed by the **client** and the **analyst**. It usually takes a while to arrive at this agreement, with the analyst asking questions until he/she is absolutely sure that he/she knows exactly what is wanted. The specification that is worked out forms the central part of the contract, defining the task fully for both parties. There are various techniques for gathering this information:
- Observing the workplace.
- Gathering all the paperwork for the existing system.
- Interviewing the client to clarify his/her needs.
- Interviewing users/employees to clarify their needs.
- Issuing questionnaires to gather ideas and opinions on the existing system.

Design stage

This is actually the hard part, but the part that often gets the least attention by novice programmers. It is at this stage that the problem is actually solved. It is only after the

Chapter 2

programmer knows exactly **what** is the problem to be solved, that he can begin to think about **how** to solve it. This phase of the development is called the **design** phase. Here the problem is broken down into 'chunks' and each 'chunk' is then broken down further and further until the little bits are easy to solve in any programming language. The solution to the problem is called the **algorithm**, a fancy word for a plan. The process of repeatedly breaking the problem into smaller and smaller steps is called 'stepwise refinement', but you are not expected to remember the term for the exam. You might choose to use a **graphical design notation** or **pseudocode** to help you to solve the problem.

Examples of graphical design notations are structure diagrams, flow charts or simple block diagrams. Structure diagrams use boxes to show how the various subtasks in the problem break down into a tree-like structure. Flow charts use different shaped boxes to show the kind of command or instruction to be used. Diamonds are used for choices (like IF), rounded rectangles are used for loops and plain boxes are used for assignments and calculations. Flow charts are very useful in showing flow of control. Simple block diagrams are used to show how the problem can be broken down.

Example

Problem
Write a program that will calculate the volume of a number of rooms. The program will first ask how many rooms there are. The program will then ask for the dimensions of the room, calculate the volume and output the volume for each room in turn.

Disadvantages
The details of each of the stages are not given in the flow chart, they will have to be described elsewhere. If this is also done graphically there will be quite a few diagrams to make sense of.

Advantages
The structure of the program is very clear. The flow of control in the program, the order of execution of blocks of code, is also clear.

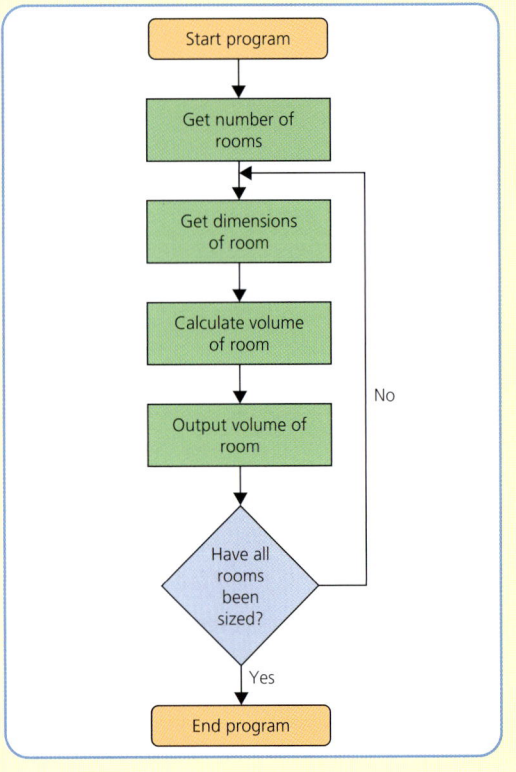

Figure 2.1 Flow chart

Pseudocode is a code-like description of the stages involved in solving the task. It is closer to English than a programming language and it helps us to write out and understand how to solve the problem. Below is a simple example of the use of pseudocode.

Example

Problem
Write a program that will calculate the volume of a number of rooms. The program will first ask how many rooms there are. The program will then ask for the dimensions of the room, calculate the volume and output the volume for each room in turn.

Algorithm in pseudocode

Main program

```
1    Ask user for the number of rooms, store in number.
2    Start of fixed loop (1 to number).
3       Ask for dimensions of room.
4       Calculate volume as length x breadth x height.
5       Display volume of room.
6    End of fixed loop.
7    End program.
```

Refinement of step 3

```
3.1  Ask for length of room, store in length.
3.2  Ask for breadth of room, store in breadth.
3.3  Ask for height of room, store in height.
```

Once the algorithm is written, it is easier to code the problem. Also, the algorithm can be passed on to another member of the team to code. The solution of the problem is not tied to any one language. The above algorithm could be implemented in True Basic, Visual Basic, Pascal, C++ or any other high level language of your choice.

Implementation phase

After the 'thinking' part is over and the design has been written, a programmer will be given the task of writing, or **implementing**, the code in a particular programming language. This might be very straightforward, just writing one line of program code for each line of pseudocode in the algorithm, or it might require a little thought as to exactly what bits of code can be used to do the task. The programmer should be careful to follow the design that is given, as he/she might only be implementing a small part of a bigger program and has to make sure that it fits properly.

The programmer also needs to make sure that the code is **readable**, in case someone else has to do something with the code at a later date. This can be done in a number of ways. Subroutines can be used to help structure the code. Variable and subroutine names should give some indication of what they hold or do. If a procedure is called *FindMaximum* it is fairly easy to work out what it does. The same is true for the following variable names: Surname$, TaxRate, PassMark, SquirrelCounter, ComputingMarks( ). Typing all of the keywords in capitals makes them stand out and aids readability. Internal documentation, or

Chapter 2

comments or remarks, can give information about what a piece of code does. Another way of making your code readable is to make effective use of white space, in the form of blank lines and/or indentation. The use of blank lines between blocks of code allows code to be grouped together logically. Indentation of the lines of code within loops or IF statements can make the structure of the code more obvious.

Below is a comparison of two programs written in True Basic. It shows how each of the above techniques aids readability and makes code easier to understand.

Poor code	Readable code

let x = 0
print "pass mark";
input a
for p = 1 to 20
print "mark";
input m
if m>=p then let x =x+1
next p
print x;"passed"
end
	!A program to count the number of passes
	!in a class of 20. All marks are percentages.
	
	LET count = 0
	
	PRINT "What is the pass mark";
	INPUT pass
	
	FOR pupil = 1 TO 20
	    PRINT "What is the mark for pupil"; pupil; "?"
	    INPUT mark
	    IF mark >= pass THEN
	        LET count = count + 1
	    END IF
	NEXT pupil
	
	PRINT "A total of"; count; "pupils passed the test."
	
	END

The left hand side is much harder to read, even in this short program. This makes it harder to understand, harder to find errors, harder to edit errors and harder to add to the program at a later stage.

Key Points

Implementation phase

- Use subroutines to structure code logically, e.g. a subroutine to FindMaximum.
- Use meaningful variable and subroutine names, e.g. find_item( ), average.
- Put all keywords/command words in CAPITALS, e.g. PRINT "Hello".
- Make effective use of white space, e.g. blank lines and indentation.
- Use clear comments at start or in code, e.g. REM Function to calculate discount.

Testing phase

Once the code has been entered, and all the typing mistakes removed, it has to be **tested** with a range of inputs to make sure that it does the job it is meant to do and that it does not keep crashing all the time. The three areas of input that have to be tested are *normal*, *extreme* and *exceptional*. These are also called 'in range', 'boundary' and 'out of range'. Below is a table of test data to test fully a subroutine validating data input as whole percentages.

Normal (in range)	Extreme (boundary)	Exceptional (out of range)
6, 21, 57, 99	0, 100	-1, 101, 69.2
(4 items between 0 and 100)	(extremes of the range)	(below, above, non-integer)

Documentation phase

When you buy a game, or any software, you usually get a manual with it. This manual is part of the **documentation** of the software. The two items of documentation that you have to know for this course are the **user guide** and the **technical guide**.

The user guide contains instructions for someone using the software, instructions on how to load and run the software and tips on how to use it.

The technical guide has the system requirements data, how much RAM and disk space is needed etc., and perhaps a list of troubleshooting tips for installing and running the software. On large software projects, such as network operating systems, it can be much larger than the user guide. It can contain a version history, a list of known bugs and software conflicts, a list of software components and details of the function library.

Evaluation phase

The last thing produced before a program is handed over to the client is a report evaluating the software. The **evaluation** of software covers three main areas in the Intermediate 2 course. These are:

- Does the program do the job it was written to do?
- Is the program easy for a user to understand and use?
- Is the actual program code easy to read?

The terms used for each of these are:

- **fitness for purpose**
- **user interface**
- **readability**.

Fitness for purpose comes from comparing what the software actually does to the list of things asked for in the analysis phase. Any claims for the software must be backed up by evidence that the software produces the correct output. This would come from the final stage of the testing phase.

The evaluation of the **user interface** will be produced by testing the software on future users and gathering opinions on its ease of use. It covers things like clarity of menus and instructions, layout of screens and dialog boxes and quality of the user guide and help files. This process is similar to the one carried out at the analysis phase.

Readability of the software would comment on the list of things described in the implementation section:

- Use of subroutines to structure code logically, e.g. a subroutine to FindMaximum.
- Meaningful variable and subroutine names, e.g. find_item( ), average.
- All keywords/command words in capitals, e.g. PRINT 'Hello'.
- Effective use of white space, e.g. blank lines and indentation.
- Use of clear comments at start or in code, e.g. REM Function to calculate discount.

The evaluation report is given to the client with the software before payment is handed over.

Maintenance phase

This stage is probably new to the way that you work because once you have handed in a finished program and it has been marked, you will probably never touch it again. Things do not happen like that in the real world! You may need to revisit the software.

This final phase of the software development process follows the shipping of the software to the client. It covers any changes to the software that have to be made after the client takes delivery of the software.

These changes may be as a result of one of the following scenarios:

- You have to come back to fix mistakes in the software not noticed during testing. This happens all the time in commercial software: think about the number of 'patches', updates and bug fixes the latest version of an operating system needs.
- The client has changed something about the hardware or software, e.g. a new printer or operating system, and they need a new version of the software that works with the new system. In larger pieces of software this can also be dealt with by writing a new driver for the hardware.
- The software works well but the client wants to add new features or to make other changes to the software. This will create a newer version of the software.

Questions

Q1 State which two stages of the software development process are missing from the list: analysis, design, testing, evaluation and maintenance.

Q2 Describe the function of the analysis and maintenance phases of the software development process.

Q3 State the purpose of pseudocode.

Q4 Name one graphical design notation and state one advantage it has over pseudocode.

Q5 Test data is being constructed for a program handling test marks as whole percentages. State two examples of each of normal, extreme and exceptional test data which should be used.

Chapter 2

Software development languages and environments

What You Should Know

About machine code and high level languages

All computers work in binary, sets of ones and zeros. Initially in computing all programs had to be written in binary.

The set of binary codes that stand for the set of commands that the computer actually understands is called **machine code**. Every family of processors has its own version of machine code. This is why a game written for the PC cannot run on a games console.

It is difficult to write machine code programs because:
- they are difficult to read and understand
- it is harder to learn the codes
- it is easier to make a mistake typing in the ones and zeros or the short codes
- these mistakes are harder to find and correct.

The next development in the writing of software was the invention of **high level languages**, like Visual Basic. These languages have a sentence-like structure and use English words as command words. High level languages make it easier for people to write and read computer programs.

Need for translators

Computers only understand binary (machine code) and so a program written in a high level language needs to be translated into binary before the computer can run the program.

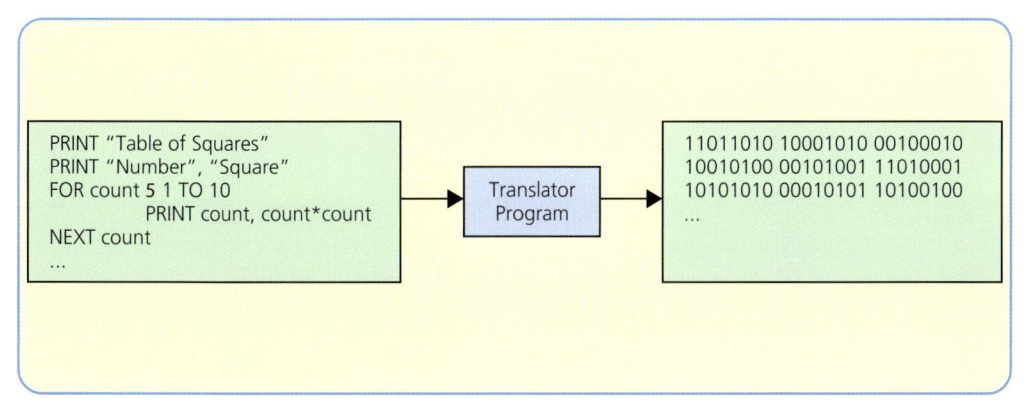

```
PRINT "Table of Squares"
PRINT "Number", "Square"
FOR count 5 1 TO 10
        PRINT count, count*count
NEXT count
...
```
→ Translator Program →
```
11011010 10001010 00100010
10010100 00101001 11010001
10101010 00010101 10100100
...
```

Figure 2.2

Types of translator program

There are two types of translator program: **interpreters** and **compilers**. They both translate the high level language program into machine code so that it can be executed. You will have used a translator program in your class work and your coursework to translate and run your programs. There are hundreds of programming languages and several of them have more

35

than one translator program you can use. You could try typing 'C++ compiler' into Google and see how many different options there are.

These translators work in different ways. An **interpreter** works by translating and then executing each line of the program in turn.

```
PRINT "Table of Squares"
PRINT "Number", "Square"
FOR count 5 1 TO 10
        PRINT count, count*count
NEXT count
...
```
Takes each line from the program in turn

Translator Program

PRINT "Table of Squares"

Translates single line then executes it!

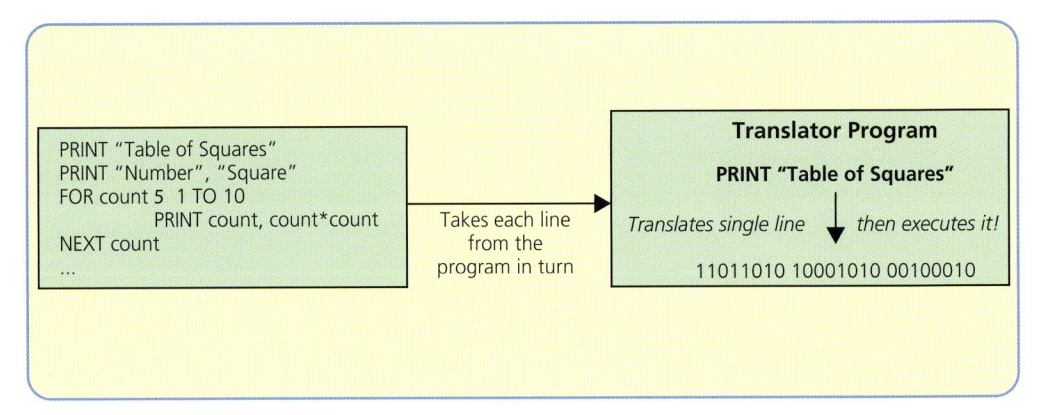

11011010 10001010 00100010

Figure 2.3

A **compiler** makes a machine code version of the program by translating each line in turn and saving it in the file. This machine code version, the '.exe' file, is then able to be run again and again without further need for translation.

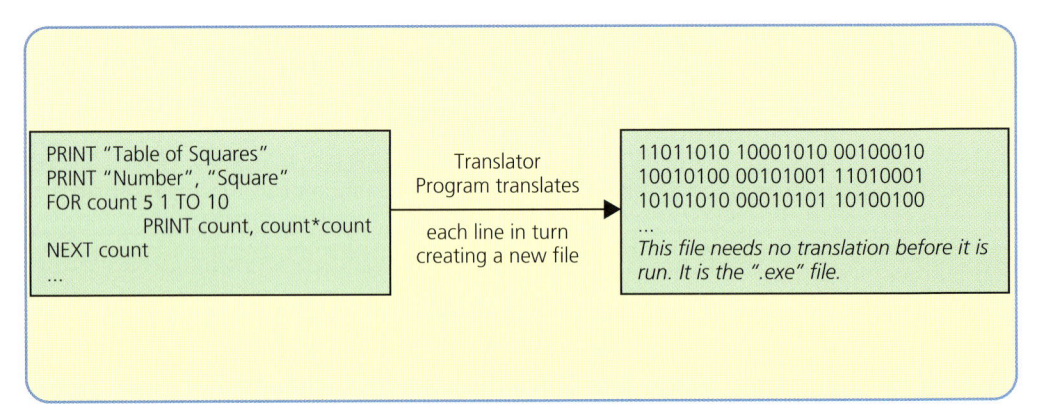

```
PRINT "Table of Squares"
PRINT "Number", "Square"
FOR count 5 1 TO 10
        PRINT count, count*count
NEXT count
...
```
Translator Program translates each line in turn creating a new file

11011010 10001010 00100010
10010100 00101001 11010001
10101010 00010101 10100100
...
This file needs no translation before it is run. It is the ".exe" file.

Figure 2.4

Advantages and disadvantages of interpreters and compilers

The **advantages** of using an **interpreter** are:

- The program will start running as soon as the first line is translated.
- A program will start to run even if it is not finished or it has errors in it.
- It is easier to spot errors during the translation/execution of the program.

The **disadvantages** of using an **interpreter** are:

- No copy of the machine code is saved, so the program will have to be translated again every time it is run.
- Commands are translated before being run, so a line in a loop is translated more than once.

- You need to have the translator program or you cannot run the program.

The **advantages** of using a **compiler** are:
- The machine code file is saved, so the program only needs to be translated once.
- The machine code file does not need to be translated, so it can be loaded and will run immediately.
- The user does not need the translator to run the machine code file.
- The lines in a loop are only translated once and then run a number of times.

The **disadvantages** of using a **compiler** are:
- You have to wait until the code is complete and the errors have been fixed before the translation can be finished and the machine code is run.
- The program has to be re-translated each time it is changed.

What is a macro?

A macro is a small program, or script, built into an application or document that will carry out a complex or frequently used function.

Macros can be written using a scripting language like Visual Basic for Applications (VBA). Here menu options and program actions are built into a small program which can be run later.

Macros can also be created by recording user actions as a series of mouse moves/clicks and menu choices. The recording is started and the user carries out the task which is to be automated. The recorded moves are then saved with an appropriate name.

Here is a screenshot from Microsoft Word showing the tools for creating macros.

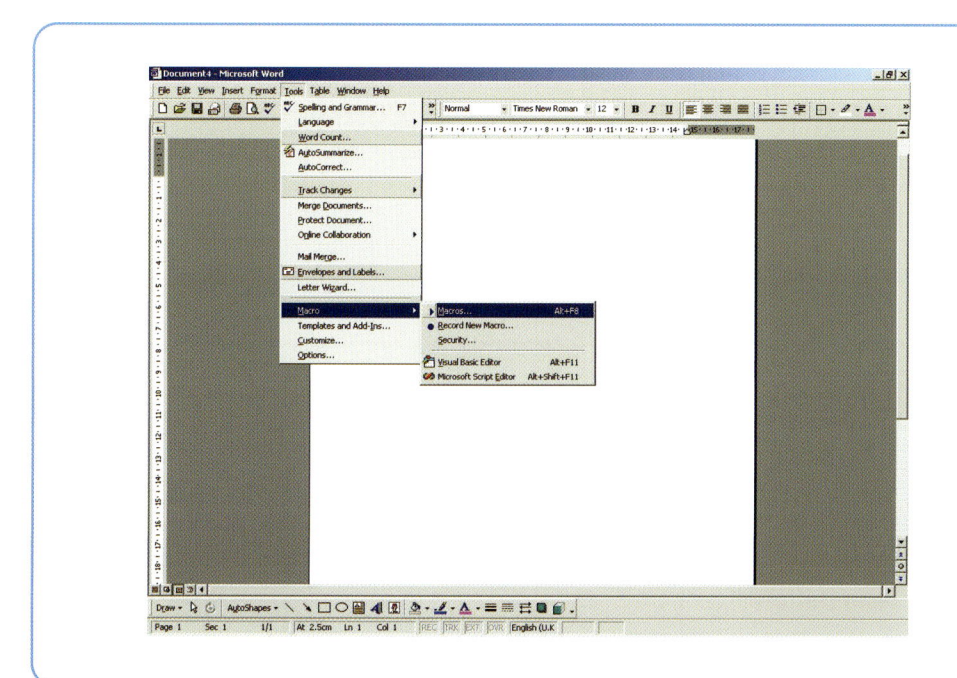

Figure 2.5

Chapter 2

Macros are then usually assigned to a single keystroke or key sequence. By pressing these 'hotkeys' the user can then run the macro, repeating the sequence recorded earlier.

There are many different macros built into Microsoft Word. They carry out several of the functions available in the menus.

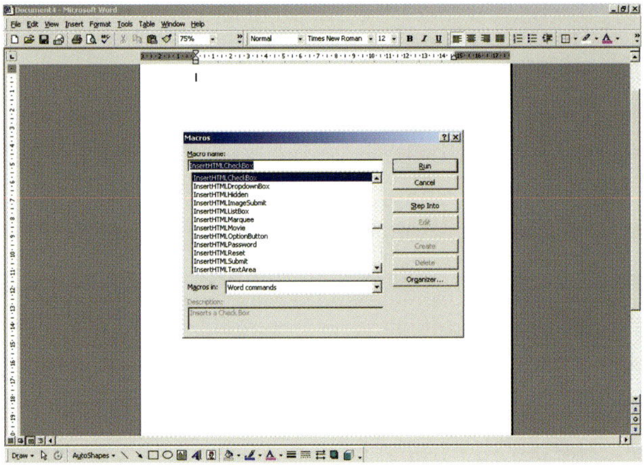

Common examples of the use of macros

Figure 2.6

There are many examples of how macros are used. Some common ones are:

- The performance of preset searches and sorts in a database.
- The creation of a mail merge.
- The importing or exporting of data from a database or spreadsheet.
- The formatting of a document.
- The inclusion of data elements such as video or sound.
- Any other complex or frequently used set of instructions or commands.

Use of a text editor in creating a program

Every translator program has a **text editor** built in. It allows you to enter, edit, format and print the program code. Sometimes the code is written in a text editor before it gets near a translator program. The creation of a web page by typing the HTML in Word, or even Notepad, is a good example of this. The code is then run by the HTML translator built into Explorer, or any other web browser.

Questions

Q6 Describe how an interpreter translates a program.

Q7 State two features of a high level language.

Q8 State the type of program that is used to type in and/or edit programs.

Chapter 2

High level programming language constructs

In the Intermediate 2 course you are expected to be able to describe, with examples, a number of programming constructs. You are also expected to be able to use each of these in classwork, within the coursework task and in the exam. The descriptions below have examples in True Basic and Visual Basic.

Variables

Any program that you write will have to store values while it works. For this we use **variables**. Think of these as labelled boxes containing values you will need to store for later use.

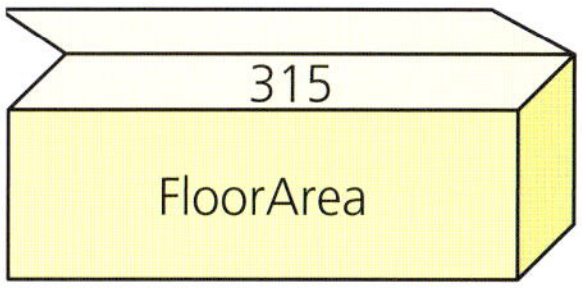

You will be working with two **data types**, to hold numbers and text. These will be held in **numeric** and **string variables**. In Higher you will learn about and use a couple more. It is good practice to follow a few simple rules when naming variables. Variable names should:

Figure 2.7

- be meaningful, describing what data is held in them, e.g. Passmark, Name
- have a dollar sign if they are holding text in True Basic, e.g. name$
- not have spaces in them (use an underscore if you need to), e.g. TaxRate, tax_rate
- not be command words or key words like FOR, IF, WHILE
- not start with a number, e.g. use Num1 instead of 1stNumber.

Input and output commands

The first program that most beginners write is the 'Hello world!' program. They would then adapt this to simple exchanges of information with the user.

True Basic	Visual Basic
! Simple input/output demo	'Simple input/output demo
PRINT "Hello world!"	PicDisplay.Print "Hello world!"
INPUT PROMPT "Enter your name":name$	Name = InputBox("Enter your name")
PRINT "Hello";name$	PicDisplay.Print "Hello" & Name
INPUT PROMPT "Enter year": year	Year = InputBox("Enter year")
PRINT "You are in year"; year	PicDisplay.Print "You are in" & Year

Note that the first line of each of the above programs is a comment, or remark, to explain what is going on to someone reading the program code.

Assignment and calculations

The other way of getting a value into a variable is **assignment**. This can happen when you set a constant value in a program or when you do calculations. Mathematical calculations use the standard arithmetical operations for add, subtract, multiply, divide and 'to the power of' (+,-,*,/,^). Brackets are used to affect the order of calculation, and the normal rules of BODMAS apply (Brackets of Division, Multiplication, Addition, Subtraction).

Chapter 2

True Basic	Visual Basic
! Assignment examples	'Assignment examples
LET school$ = "Balwearie"	School = "Bannerman"
LET radius = 12	Radius = 12
LET circumference = 2 * 3.14 * radius	Circumference = 2 * 3.14 * Radius
LET area = 3.14 * radius ^ 2	Area = 3.14 * Radius ^ 2
LET celsius = (fahrenheit – 32) / 9 * 5	Celsius = (Fahrenheit – 32) / 9 * 5

Fixed loops

When you have a piece of code that you want the computer to repeat a set number of times you would use a **fixed loop**, sometimes called a FOR … NEXT loop. A loop is often referred to as an *iterative* control structure. The FOR command sets up a control variable with an initial value, usually 1. The NEXT command adds a number, again usually 1, to that variable and the loop stops when the upper limit is reached. In simple terms the following code makes the computer repeat the lines in the loop 10 times.

Example

FOR number = 1 TO 10

…

NEXT number

In the first example below the program prints out the 4× table using the value of the control variable (num) in the calculation.

True Basic	Visual Basic
! Fixed Loop examples	'Fixed Loop examples
LET table = 4	Table = 4
PRINT "This is the" ;table; "times table"	PicDisplay.Print "This is the" & Table & "times table"
FOR num = 1 TO 10	FOR num = 1 TO 10
LET answer = num * table	Ans = num * Table
PRINT num;"*";table;"is";answer	PicDisplay.Print num & "*" & Table & "is" & Ans
NEXT num	NEXT num

In the second example the loop counts down by one, as the STEP command changes the value to be added to the control variable.

True Basic	Visual Basic
!Countdown example using STEP	'Countdown example using STEP
FOR count = 10 TO 0 STEP -1	FOR count = 10 TO 0 STEP -1
PRINT count	PicDisplay.Print count
NEXT count	NEXT count
PRINT "Blast Off!"	PicDisplay.Print "Blast Off!"

One-dimensional (1-D) arrays

If you want to hold a set of values of the same data type you would use an **array**. This can be thought of as a row of boxes, each containing a value. It is called a 1-D array because it is only one row of boxes. If you study Computing to Advanced Higher you will use 2-D (or larger) arrays.

A value in an array can be accessed by using the name of the array and the number of the box. In Figure 2.8, the command PRINT TestMarks(1) prints out the value 8.

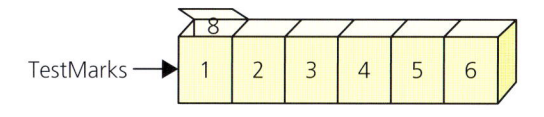

Figure 2.8

True Basic	Visual Basic
!Code for filling an array	'Code for filling an array
DIM marks(10)	Dim Marks(5) As Integer
LET total = 0	Total = 0
FOR n = 1 TO 10	FOR n = 1 TO 10
PRINT "Enter mark"; n;	Marks(n) = InputBox("Enter mark" & n)
INPUT marks(n)	
LET total = total + marks(n)	Total = Total + Marks(n)
NEXT n	NEXT n
PRINT "The total was"; total	PicDisplay.Print "The total was"& total

Conditional statements (IF)

A **conditional statement** is a way of making a choice in a programming language. A simple IF statement allows you to choose to do or not to do an action. Groups of actions can be contained in IF statements and, by using IF…THEN…ELSE, you can choose one 'branch' over another. The code in the following table gives examples of each of these three uses of IF.

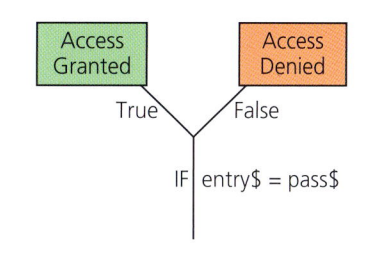

Figure 2.9

SOFTWARE DEVELOPMENT

Chapter 2

41

Chapter 2

True Basic	Visual Basic
INPUT PROMPT "Enter your age ":age	Age = InputBox("Enter your age")
!Simple IF	'Simple IF
IF age < 18 THEN PRINT "You cannot vote"	IF (Age < 18) THEN PicDisplay.Print "You cannot vote"
!Simple IF with more then one action	'Simple IF with more then one action
IF age < 17 THEN	IF (Age < 17) THEN
PRINT "You cannot drive a car"	PicDisplay.Print "You cannot drive a car"
PRINT "Check about mopeds"	PicDisplay.Print "Check about mopeds"
END IF	ENDIF
!Simple IF with two branches, using ELSE	'Simple IF with two branches (IF..THEN..ELSE)
IF age < 17 THEN	IF (Age < 17) THEN
PRINT "You cannot drive a car"	PicDisplay.Print "You cannot drive a car"
ELSE	ELSE
PRINT "Get your provisional licence"	PicDisplay.Print "Get your provisional licence"
PRINT "Invest in some driving lessons"	PicDisplay.Print "Invest in some driving lessons"
END IF	ENDIF

Conditional loops

It may be that you want to do something more than once, but you don't know how often you will need to do it. Here is where the **conditional loop** comes in. This will allow you to set a condition to allow the program to leave the loop. There are a few versions of this type of loop in True Basic. They can each be useful, but most programmers tend to stick to one type and bend the conditions to fit!

Chapter 2

SOFTWARE DEVELOPMENT

True Basic	Visual Basic

!Post-conditioned loop exiting on true result
DO
  INPUT PROMPT "Enter password":pass$
LOOP UNTIL pass$ = "fruitbat"
	'Post-conditioned loop exiting on true result
	DO
	  Pass = InputBox("Enter password")
	LOOP UNTIL Pass = "fruitbat"

!Post-conditioned loop exiting on false result
DO
  INPUT PROMPT "Enter password":pass$
LOOP WHILE pass$ <> "fruitbat"
	!Pre-conditioned loop exiting on false result
	DO WHILE Cash < Total
	  PicDisplay.Print "You still owe" & (Total – Cash)
	  Pay = InputBox("How much do you want to pay now")
	  Cash = Cash + Pay
	LOOP

!Pre-conditioned loop exiting on true result
DO UNTIL cash = total
  PRINT "You owe"; total – cash
  PRINT "How much do you want to pay now";
  INPUT pay
  LET cash = cash + pay
LOOP	

!Pre-conditioned loop exiting on false result
DO WHILE cash <> total
  PRINT "You owe"; total – cash
  PRINT "How much do you want to pay now";
  INPUT pay
  LET cash = cash + pay
LOOP	

Complex conditions and the logical operators

The IF statements and conditional loops above were described as 'simple', which referred to the exit condition relying on **one** thing being true or false. Complex conditions can depend on two or more things.

These conditions can be combined using the keywords AND, OR and NOT.

- For the whole **AND** condition to be **true**, **both** parts have to be **true**.
- For the whole **OR** condition to be **true**, **either** part can be **true**.
- For the **NOT** to be **true**, the condition it applies to must be **false**.

To give an example of the difference between each of these, the blue area in diagram A represents those pupils in a class who are female AND have blue eyes (the blue-eyed females only). The blue area in diagram O represents those pupils in the class who are female OR have blue eyes (every female plus the blue-eyed boys). Diagram N shows those pupils who have blue eyes AND who are NOT female (the blue-eyed boys).

43

Chapter 2

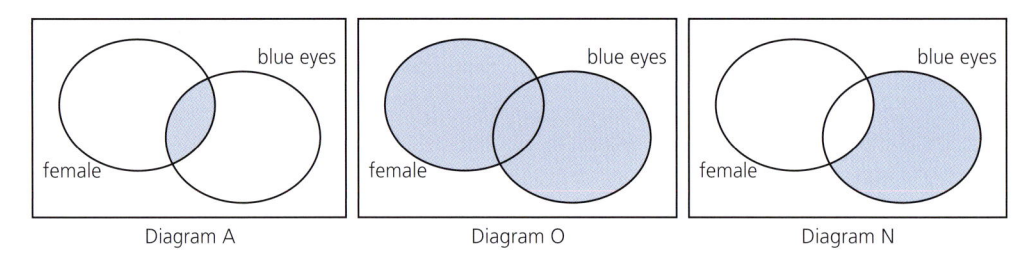

Diagram A   Diagram O   Diagram N

Figure 2.10

The following examples of code illustrate the use of AND, OR and NOT.

True Basic	Visual Basic
INPUT PROMPT "Enter your age":age	Age = InputBox("Enter your age")

IF age >= 17 AND age <= 70 THEN
   PRINT "You can donate blood"
END IF
	IF (Age >= 17 AND Age <= 70) THEN
	   PicDisplay.Print "You can donate blood"
	ENDIF

IF age < 17 OR age > 70 THEN
   PRINT "You cannot donate blood"
END IF
	IF (Age < 17 OR Age > 70) THEN
	   PicDisplay.Print "You cannot donate blood"
	ENDIF

IF NOT(age >= 17) THEN
   PRINT "You are too young to donate"
END IF
	IF NOT(Age >= 17) THEN
	   PicDisplay.Print "You are too young to donate"
	ENDIF

Nested loops

It is sometimes necessary to place one loop inside another. This is technique is called 'nesting'. The two examples opposite show how nested loops can be used to help work out the average mark in each of the three NAB assessments for a class of 20 pupils.

True Basic	Visual Basic
!Nested loop example	'Nested loop example
DIM marks(3)	DIM Marks(3) as Single
FOR test = 1 TO 3	FOR test = 1 TO 3
PRINT "Now entering marks for NAB"; test	PicDisplay.Print "Now entering marks for NAB"& test
FOR pupil = 1 to 20	FOR pupil = 1 to 20
PRINT "Enter mark for pupil"; pupil	Mark = InputBox("Enter mark for pupil"& pupil)
INPUT mark	LET Marks(test) = Marks(test) + Mark
LET marks(test) = marks(test) + mark	NEXT pupil
NEXT pupil	LET marks(test) = marks(test)/20
LET marks(test) = marks(test)/20	PicDisplay.Print "Ave for NAB"& test &"="&marks(test)
PRINT "Ave for NAB" ;test; "="; marks(test)	NEXT test
NEXT test	

Description and exemplification of pre-defined functions

A **pre-defined function** is a section of code that has been written, checked, tested, translated and saved in a function library for later use by other programmers. It may be used for data handling, mathematical/statistical functions or many other functions. There are many useful pre-defined functions in any programming language, and a few from True Basic are given below (there may be slight grammar differences in Visual Basic so check with your teacher):

- RND gives a random real number between 0 and 1.
- RANDOMIZE gives a new random number each time RND is used.
- INT(grade) takes the value in the variable, here called grade, and drops the numbers after decimal point, i.e. INT(3.87) has the value 3.
- ROUND(num) rounds a number to the nearest whole number.
- ROUND(num,2) rounds a number to two decimal places.
- LEN(string$) returns the length of the variable or piece of text passed into the function, i.e. LEN("fruitbat") returns the value 8.

Below is a worked example in True Basic and Visual Basic which uses the random number generation and INT functions to analyse the frequency of random numbers.

True Basic Standard Functions	Visual Basic Standard Functions
! Frequency of 10000 dice rolls	'Frequency of 10000 dice rolls
DIM rolls(6)	DIM rolls(6) as Integer
RANDOMIZE	RANDOMIZE
FOR dice = 1 TO 10000	FOR Dice = 1 TO 10000
LET roll = INT(RND*6)+1	Roll = INT(RND*6)+1
LET rolls(roll) = rolls(roll) + 1	Rolls(Roll) = Rolls(Roll) + 1
NEXT dice	NEXT Dice
FOR num = 1 TO 6	FOR Num = 1 TO 6
PRINT num ;"rolled"; rolls(num);"times"	PicDisplay.Print Num &"rolled"& Rolls(Num)&"times"
NEXT num	NEXT Num

Chapter 2

Questions

Q9 Using a programming language of your choice, write a complex condition to identify a number in the range 18 to 30.

Q10 Describe what is meant by a nested loop.

Q11 Describe the data type and data structure that would be needed to store a list of ten surnames.

Q12 Name the standard algorithm that would be used to find the name "Carrick" in this list.

Q13 State one example of a pre-defined function.

Q14 Explain why the use of pre-defined functions might speed up the creation of a program.

Standard algorithms

You are expected to be able to recognise which of the four standard algorithms is appropriate to use in a given situation. The four standard algorithms are:

- Input validation – for validating that input is within a given range.
- Find min/max – for finding the smallest/largest value in a list/array.
- Count occurrences – for counting how many times a given value is in a list/array.
- Linear search – for finding a given value in a list/array.

There has been an example of this type of question in every exam, including every Higher Computing exam when it was part of that course. The trick is to read the question carefully and figure out which algorithm is required in the scenario. Watch out for simple errors like wrongly using find max to find the best time in a race – the winner usually has the shortest time!

You are not expected to be able to describe any of these algorithms in any great detail, except for input validation. You have to be able to write pseudocode and actual program code for this algorithm. The algorithm is very straightforward.

Algorithm for input validation

- Start conditional loop
-    Ask for number between 0 and 100
-    Store number in variable
-    IF number is outside range
-       Display error message
-    End IF
- End conditional loop when number is within range

Chapter 2

There are two versions of the code for this algorithm, one for decimal numbers and one for whole numbers.

The actual True Basic and Visual Basic code for each of these is shown below.

True Basic	Visual Basic
!Code for validating a number between 0 and 100	'Code for validating a number between 0 and 100
DO	DO
INPUT PROMPT "Enter your mark":mark	Mark = InputBox("Enter your mark")
IF mark > 100 OR mark < 0 THEN	IF Mark > 100 OR Mark < 0 THEN
PRINT "Error. Please re-enter mark."	PicDisplay.Print "Error. Please re-enter mark."
END IF	ENDIF
LOOP UNTIL mark >= 0 AND mark <= 100	LOOP UNTIL Mark >= 0 AND Mark <= 100
!Code for validating die roll between 1 and 6	'Code for validating die roll between 1 and 6
DO	DO
INPUT PROMPT "Enter your roll":d	D = InputBox("Enter your roll")
IF d > 6 OR d < 1 OR d <> INT(d) THEN	IF D > 6 OR D < 1 OR D <> INT(D) THEN
PRINT "Error. Please re-enter roll."	PicDisplay.Print "Error. Please re-enter roll."
END IF	ENDIF
LOOP UNTIL d >= 1 AND d <= 6 AND d = INT(d)	LOOP UNTIL D >= 1 AND D <= 6 AND D = INT(D)

Questions

Q15 The subroutine calculates the fastest time in the array holding the 100m results. Name the standard algorithm used here.

Q16 Explain the term 'fitness for purpose'.

Q17 Describe how 'readability' would support the testing stage.

Q18 State two ways of improving the readability of a program.

Q19 Name the two items of documentation produced at the documentation stage.

Chapter 3

COMPUTER NETWORKING

Network applications

The world wide web (WWW)

The **world wide web** is made up of multimedia web pages that are stored on computers across the world. Web pages hold text, sounds, graphics, animations, and videos. These are linked together by **hyperlinks**.

A hyperlink appears either as underlined text such as Computing Revision or as a graphic, like the one shown here. Clicking on a hyperlink instructs the browser to fetch a web page and display it.

Figure 3.1

The web browser

You find and view web pages using a web browser. A browser is a program that helps you navigate the world wide web. You use a browser to move between and look at web pages. You can enter the address of the page you want to go to or you can click on a hyperlink.

A browser will remember where pages are, once the address is added to the **bookmarks favourites** list.

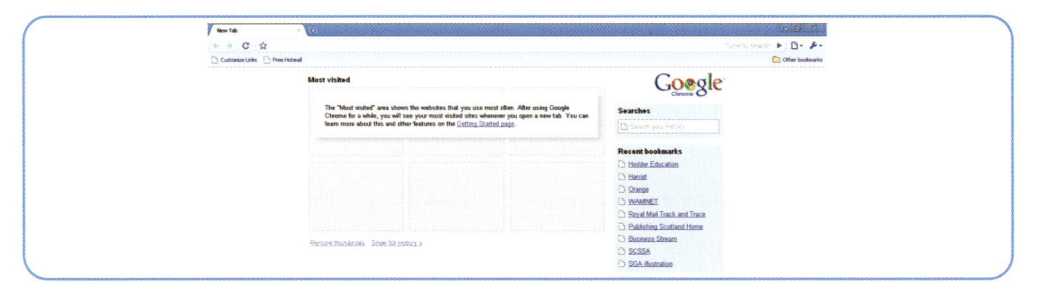

Figure 3.2 A web browser

Features of a web browser

The web browser allows the user to:

- find and look at web pages
- navigate between web pages and websites
- move backwards and forwards between web pages using the back and forward buttons
- remember the location of your favourite pages
- remember which pages you have visited using the 'history' function.

URL

Every web page has a unique address called a **universal resource locator (URL)**, for example http://www.bbc.co.uk.

This is divided into three parts.

The first part is the protocol. The most common one is **http**. This stands for **hypertext transfer protocol**. It is used in transferring web pages to your computer. Some URLs begin with **ftp**. This stands for **File Transfer Protocol** and is used to transfer files across the Internet.

The second part indicates which server the web page is stored on, for example **www.bbc**.

The third part indicates the type of organisation that is storing the web pages, for example, **co.uk** for a company in the UK. Here are some examples of the third part of the URL:

Third part of URL	Type of organisation
.sch	School
.com	Commercial company
.net	Network organisation
.mil	Military
.org	An organisation
.gov	Government organisation
.ac	An academic organisation such as a university or college

Accessing the Internet using a mobile phone

You no longer need a laptop or a desktop to access the services on the Internet. You can now use a mobile phone as long as it has a special protocol called **Wireless Application Protocol (WAP).** WAP enables web content to be delivered over the mobile phone networks. Using WAP phones you can collect and send email as well as browse for information.

Microbrowsers

Microbrowsers are browsers that allow mobile phones to send and receive email and browse the web. They can't do everything a browser on your desktop can. The interactivity and full multimedia features of web pages are unavailable in microbrowsers.

Figure 3.3

Chapter 3

Electronic mail (email)

The most widely used service on the Internet is electronic mail. Electronic mail allows the user to send and receive electronic messages to or from anyone anywhere in the world who has access to the Internet.

Email addresses

Email addresses have three parts. For example, JoeSoap@yahoo.co.uk.

Joe Soap	@yahoo	.co.uk
This is the name of the person.	This is the email server which manages his email.	This is the type of organisation that owns the server.

Email features

Here is list of common email features: read, save, delete, print, reply, write, attach files, send, store addresses, organise messages into folders.

Advantages of email

- Speed of delivery compared with surface mail.
- Low cost compared with surface mail.
- You can sent attachments, documents or pictures, around the world.
- Ability to check mail from any network workstation or Internet connection.
- Security: mail is protected by IDs and passwords.
- Ability to send multiple copies of mail at one time.
- Ability to store and organise messages.

Disadvantages of email

There are a number of problems with the growing use of email.

- Email attachments can contain **viruses**.
- **Junk mail**, known as SPAM, arrives by email.
- **Disk space** is wasted by people who do not delete email.
- It is difficult to monitor the **content** of attachments.

File transfer

Attachments

The most common way to transfer a file across the Internet is to attach it to an email. The process of attaching a file is straightforward, usually just a click to select the file for transfer.

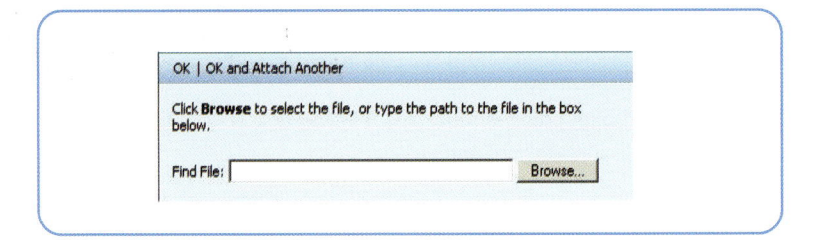

Figure 3.4

Email providers do put limits on the size and number of files that can be attached to emails, for example, maximum of 10 MB per message. Attachments are sometimes used to send viruses. Unexpected attachments must be treated with care.

File transfer protocol

You can also transfer files using **File Transfer Protocol** (**FTP**). You can visit an FTP site and, after you have logged in, download any file stored on the site or upload a file of your own. FTP sites are used to transfer programs, data files including music files. The URL for an FTP site will start with ftp//:.

ISP

An Internet Service Provider (ISP) is a business which provides users with access to the Internet for a fee. The ISP issues a unique user ID and password. You then use the user ID and password to log on to your ISP's computer which then helps you access the Internet.

The ISP computer:

- works with your browser to fetch web pages
- provides web-based email and messaging services
- gives access to newsgroups and chat rooms
- gives users space to store their own web pages.

Go to this website http://www.allthebrands.co.uk and put in the search term 'ISP' to see a list of providers.

Search engines

Search engines are used to look for web pages. A simple search has one item or topic in the search, for example, 'Computer Network LAN'.

The search engine will find all the web pages related to that topic and send the results to your computer for your browser to display them.

You must be careful how you construct searches as it often only looks for the words and not the phrase. For example, the above search would display the pages with the whole phrase, but also any page with one or more of the words in them.

There are millions of pages on the Internet with the word 'computer' in them!

Figure 3.5

Chapter 3

> ### Questions
>
> **Q1** Which program do you use to find your way around the Internet?
>
> **Q2** Here is a URL: http://www.visit-fortwilliam.co.uk. Describe the three parts of this URL.
>
> **Q3** List three features of a web browser.
>
> **Q4** What is a 'microbrowser'?
>
> **Q5** Describe a limitation of a 'microbrowser'.
>
> **Q6** List two advantages and two disadvantages of email.
>
> **Q7** Describe three services which an ISP provides.

E-commerce

E-commerce is the use of the Internet to carry out business. This might mean buying or selling goods or services.

E-commerce is divided into the following categories:

- **E-business** – buying and selling using networks to sell products; transmit financial details to main office; advertise; connect workers to work together on projects.
- **E-marketing** – advertising, especially on the Internet, for example, pop up adverts, spam email, giving online quotes for jobs and goods.
- **E-sales** – using the Internet to buy and pay for goods via, for example, Amazon the bookseller, or online auctions like eBay.
- **E-government** – local and national governments using the Internet to keep people informed and to ask for feedback on ideas and proposals.

Advantages

- Lower costs: there is no need for shops or people to work in them. Advertising costs are also reduced.
- Speed: orders can be taken and dealt with instantly. This is an advantage for both the customer and the business.
- People can work from home saving on the time and cost of travelling to work.

Disadvantages

- Cuts down the number of shops in the high street.
- Fewer jobs available in shops.
- Cost of setting up and maintaining a website.

Converging technologies

Computer technologies are coming together with products we use in our everyday lives.

Most of the electronic goods which we use at home, such as washing machines, DVD players and TV sets, have microchips in them.

Chapter 3

We can use digital televisions to send emails; mobile phones can send and receive emails; fridges, cookers, central heating and alarm systems can be linked into your home network. This means you can control all these devices from your desktop or even, using the Internet, from just about anywhere!

What does the growth of networks and the Internet mean for education?

- All schools, colleges and universities use networks to communicate using email, to store and share data files, to share software and hardware.
- Students have access to a wealth of network-based information. This can really boost their learning opportunities.
- Staff can use networks to communicate with students and other staff and keep up with their administration, such as keeping student records up to date.

Disadvantage
The financial cost of setting up and maintaining a network can be very high.

What does the growth of networks and the Internet mean for business?

Businesses can:
- reach customers around the world
- send accounts/customer data back to a head office anywhere in the world
- transfer money across networks
- share information and communicate across the business organisation.

Businesses must:
- pay attention to the Data Protection Act
- have excellent network security systems.

Key Points

Regulation of Investigatory Powers (RIP) Act
This Act gives the government the powers to:
- intercept communications
- acquire communications data (e.g. billing data)
- set up intrusive surveillance (on residential premises/in private vehicles)
- set up covert surveillance in the course of specific operations
- use covert human intelligence sources (agents, informants, undercover officers)
- access encrypted data.

Code of conduct

All schools, colleges and businesses have some sort of code of conduct which sets out guidelines that people should follow when using a network. This is often called an 'Acceptable Use Policy'.

COMPUTER NETWORKING

Chapter 3

This code of conduct sets out guidelines to make sure that people's use of the network stays within laws such as the Data Protection Act and the Designs and Copyright Act. A good code will also give guidelines about how to respect other people and their rights when using the network, for example, banning the use of the network to send chain-mail, hate-mail or other offensive materials.

Questions

Q8 Give two advantages of e-commerce:

(a) for the user

(b) for a business.

Q9 What does 'converging technologies' mean? Give two examples.

Q10 Give two examples of what the growth of networks means for:

(a) education

(b) business.

Q11 List two key points of the RIP Act.

Q12 What sort of things are in a network code of conduct?

Network security

Physical security

To protect against unauthorised access, you can use **physical** security such as:

- security locks on the doors and windows of computer rooms
- locks on workstations themselves
- no removeable backing storage available, such as CD drives.

Software security

Probably the most used software security method requires the user to 'log on'. This involves entering a **user name** and a **password**. Passwords are stored in a database on the network. When you log in, the system looks for your password. If it finds it in the database you are given access to the network.

To protect against unauthorised access to networks or data, the following methods can be used:

- Use unique **IDs** to identify users.
- Use **passwords**.
- Password protect individual files if they contain sensitive data.
- Have multi-level **access rights**, where some people only get partial access.
- Use **biometric systems**, like fingerprint or retinal scanners.

◆ **Data encryption**: data that is encrypted is changed using a special code that is meaningless to anyone that doesn't have the **software key** which will turn the data back into its original form.

Filtering of content

Unfortunately there are many web pages that are offensive, for example, pages containing foul language or violent material.

Schools, businesses and parents use filtering software to prevent people accessing these pages.

Filtering software checks the content of web pages and blocks those that are not suitable.

> ### What You Should Know
>
> #### About Threats to Networks
> The threats to networks you need to know about are: hardware failure, software failure, data transmission failure and physical disasters.
>
> #### Hardware failure
> Servers, hard drives, routers, network interface cards, modems, cabling, wireless receivers and transmitters can all fail and cause the network to collapse.
>
> #### Software failure
> Software faults can also bring down a network: the network operating system can fail, browsers can develop faults, the database with the passwords needed for logging onto the network can become corrupted.
>
> #### Data transmission failure
> Cables can be damaged, wireless signals can suffer from interference.
>
> #### Physical disasters
> Fires, floods, burst pipes, cuts in electrical supply.

The need for backup strategy

The data stored on networks needs to be backed up constantly in case it is lost or damaged. Every day multiple copies need to be made of all important data. These copies should then be stored in a safe location. If any data is lost then it can be recovered from the backup copies.

Chapter 3

Questions

Q13 Describe three types of physical security and three types of software security.

Q14 Explain what a data transmission failure is.

Q15 Complete this table:

Topic	Description	Why it is needed
Internet content filtering		
Backup strategy		
Encryption		

Key Points

Data Transmission

Unicast
Unicast is used when sending data from one system on a network to one other specific system on a network.

Broadcast
Broadcast is used to send data to all workstations connected to a network.

Multicast
Sending a single message to a group of people at the same time, e.g. an email message sent to all the people on a distribution, or contact, list.

Voice and data transmission across networks

Besides being used to transmit data, network communications links can be used to send voice transmissions. It is now quite common for people to use networks to speak to people. All you need is the correct software and a microphone and speakers. Check out SKYPE at www.skype.com.

Wireless communication

Wireless personal area network (WPAN)

A WPAN is a wireless network that is typically limited to a small area like an office or a home. Mobile phones, mobile computers and other portable hand-held devices allow an individual to transfer data to and from a desktop system or to send data to a peripheral like a printer.

At home a WPAN can be used to communicate with fridges, cookers, central heating and alarm systems linked into the home network.

Wireless local area network (WLAN)

This is a local area network which uses wireless signals to link the computers on the network. WLANs use radio signals (Bluetooth) or infra-red (IrDA) to pass data without wires. They have many advantages as there is no need for cables, so you can move around anywhere in the office or home and still connect with the network. Wireless LAN needs a wireless transmitter, and each station on the network needs a wireless Network Interface Card (NIC).

Wireless wide area network (WWAN)

Wireless WAN can use direct satellite connections or have cellular technology built into them so that they can tap directly into the mobile phone network to link computers over great distances. Advantage: they are cheaper than using leased lines. Disadvantage: the transmission can be subject to interference.

Types of Internet connection

Type of Internet connection	Description	Bandwidth
Dialup	◆ Ordinary modem and telephone line. ◆ Mainly for light home use or occasional remote access to servers.	56 Kbps
Cable modem	◆ Data is sent through a cable television network instead of telephone lines. ◆ Instant connection: no dialling needed. ◆ Suitable for use by residential customers and home-based businesses.	Check out the latest bandwidths and prices at www.broadband checker.co.uk/.
Leased line	◆ A permanent, dedicated, connection from one point to another leased from a telecommunication company. ◆ Digital circuits known as T-carriers or T-lines are often leased. ◆ They are very expensive. ◆ Used by large businesses that need a high-speed, dedicated, always online, communications channel.	The transmission rates of T-lines are as follows: T-1 1.544 Mbps T-2 6.312 Mbps T-3 44.736 Mbps T-4 274.760 Mbps
ISDN	◆ A form of dialup digital transmission service which uses the ordinary telephone lines. ◆ A cheaper alternative to T-carrier leased lines, once popular with small businesses and domestic users.	Basic rate interface ISDN = 2 × 64 Kbps = 128 Kbps and 1 × 16 Kbps (for control information).

Chapter 3

Type of Internet Connection	Description	Bandwidth
ADSL known as broadband	◆ Uses ordinary phone lines to provide broadband access to homes and businesses. **Advantages**: ◆ Simultaneous transmission of voice and data over a single phone line. ◆ High transfer rates. ◆ Instant on connection. **Useful for**: ◆ Home use, particularly telecommuting. ◆ Small businesses which don't need expensive leased lines.	Check out the latest broadband speeds and prices at: www.broadband-finder.co.uk and www.broadbandchecker.co.uk.

Broadband

Broadband is used to describe *high-speed* transmission. It is usually used to describe ADSL and cable transmission. The definition of what high speed is varies as the technology advances.

Hardware for a wireless LAN

To be able to use a wireless local area network, the network requires a receiver and transmitter, and each computer needs a wireless network interface card.

Key Points

Domain names, domain name system and host name resolution

Domain name

A domain name is an organisation's unique name on the Internet, e.g. passexams.com.

DNS

The domain name system (DNS) is used to change the domain name into its associated address which is then used to find that organisation on the Internet. For example: passexams.com could be changed to 104.63.40.12

Host name resolution

The process of changing the **domain name** into an Internet address is known as **host name resolution**.

Chapter 3

Questions

Q16 Describe the key differences between broadcast, unicast and multicast.

Q17 Copy and complete this table:

A WPAN is	
A WLAN is	
A WWAN is	

Q18 Describe two key differences between the following ways of connecting to the Internet: a cable modem connection and a broadband ADSL connection.

Q19 Copy and complete this table:

A domain name is	
The domain name system is	
Host name resolution is	

Chapter 4

ARTIFICIAL INTELLIGENCE

The development of artificial intelligence

What is intelligence?

The study of artificial intelligence (AI) is also the study of the way we think. There are two types of person working in AI: those who are trying to get machines to imitate the way we think, and those who believe we can teach machines to think. It does not matter which of these you are, you have first to understand how humans think.

If you were trying to decide what sort of human behaviour clearly demonstrated the presence of intelligence, which would you choose? Over the past century many have tried to define human intelligence. For them intelligence is the ability to:

- solve problems
- communicate knowledge
- learn or adapt to new situations
- remember or retain knowledge
- see patterns in a confused situation
- create new ideas by combining old ideas in new ways.

There are many different views on what is intelligent behaviour so that makes it very difficult to agree on how to measure the presence of artificial intelligence. The easiest test of whether a system has AI is, can it do a task that, if it were to be done by a human, would require intelligence?

The Turing test

One of the best tests of this type was described by the British mathematician and AI pioneer Alan Turing. The Turing test is actually very simple. You take a person and sit them at a computer. This computer is connected to the AI system being tested and also to a human. The tester types a series of questions at the keyboard for each to answer. If the tester cannot tell which set of answers come from the human and which from the machine then the machine has passed the test and is said to be 'intelligent'.

Alan Turing imagined a conversation that was not limited to a narrow area and could range across many topics such as literature, music and current affairs. The simpler versions of the Turing test are not that ambitious, allowing the questions to be limited to a specific area. There is actually a prize for the first program to pass the full Turing test! Try using the Internet to find out more about the Turing test.

Early research and game playing

Early AI research often looked at writing programs that could play simple games, like noughts and crosses (OXO) or draughts (checkers in the USA).

Chapter 4

ARTIFICIAL INTELLIGENCE

Figure 4.1 The Turing test

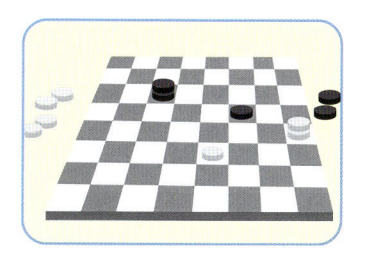

Figure 4.2

The reason these were chosen was that they had a **narrow domain**, **defined start and end points** and a **clear set of rules** for playing. They also match many of the criteria for human intelligence outlined at the start of this chapter. The Internet is a good place to look for more detail on AI and game playing.

As researchers have improved their AI techniques, the games have also improved. In 1992 a program called Chinook won the US Checkers Open Championship. It then went on to beat the World Checkers Champion in two games – although she did win the match.

Chess is, for many people, an ultimate test of intelligence. In 1997, the AI program Deep Blue beat Garry Kasparov, arguably the best chess player in history. Deep Blue did this by being able to examine 200 million possible moves in a second! Is this really a measure of intelligence?

How have developments in hardware supported AI?

The triumph of Deep Blue over Kasparov would not have been possible if it were not for the many improvements in technology over the past few decades. Every year memory chips get bigger, faster and cheaper. Backing storage has also become cheaper, larger and faster. This allows much more data to be accessed faster and therefore more complex problems to be attempted. Processors can double in power in as little as 18 months. Faster processors mean that even complex problems are able to be solved in a meaningful time. Just take a look at some computer magazines from three years ago and see how far the hardware has come.

Chapter 4

Natural language processing (NLP)

Another area of study is **natural language processing (NLP)**. This is where we try to get a computer to communicate with a human using text or the spoken word.

This is not an easy task. If we are using the written word, the text is usually scanned and then OCR (optical character recognition) software produces editable text in the form of whole words to be processed. If the message is spoken then it is recorded and that recording is broken up into individual sounds, called phonemes. These are grouped into words for processing. Either way we now have a list of words to be processed.

There are a number of problems to be overcome when processing the data to work out what the message means. These include:

- similar sounding words, e.g. hare, hair (what would you brush with a harebrush?)
- same text different meaning, e.g. lead dog (drag it along), lead dog (heavy metal)
- ambiguity of meaning, e.g. I saw her duck. Man eating fish
- Slang or technical terms, e.g. it was a solid paper, she had some liquid paper
- new words entering the language, e.g. emo girl, bling
- changing meanings, e.g. fax, text and email are all now things you do.

After the meaning has been extracted from the text, the system will work out a response and deliver it as text or using a synthesised voice. The system could provide control signals for other voice-activated hardware.

Two early examples of NLP programs are **Eliza** and **Parry**. These were both originally designed as training tools for psychologists/psychiatrists. Each works in a similar way. They follow the process above to generate responses.

Parry acts as a patient suffering from delusional paranoia; this helps train therapists in what *not* to say to a real patient!

Eliza acts as a therapist. It asks a question, analyses your response, picks out key words and asks another question to 'find out more'. An example of the type of conversation is given below:

Example

Conversation with Eliza

Person: I don't like Mondays.
Eliza: Tell me why you don't like Mondays.
Person: I have to get up earlier on a Monday.
Eliza: Why do you have to get up earlier on a Monday?
Person: I have to go to school.
Eliza: Tell me more about school.
Person: I don't want to.
Eliza: Why don't you want to talk about school?
Person: I am unhappy there.
Eliza: What is making you unhappy?
…

The message is first captured, by microphone or keyboard. It is then interpreted and the meaning discovered. An appropriate response is then generated, on screen or via speakers. Eliza is looking at the sentence structure and picking out key phrases such as 'don't like'. It then turns the statement into a question aimed at getting more information. If it does not see a way to do this, it will use a phrase like 'tell me more'.

The first attempts at these were rather limited, as you can see, but modern versions are much more realistic. The modern programs are called **chatterbots** and they are being applied in many situations. You might have already used one without knowing it.

Companies use them to answer simple email queries on websites because they appear more personal. They can be made to look 'human' and can even deal with slang. Have a look on the Internet for 'A.L.I.C.E.', 'nativeminds' or other 'chatterbots'.

Figure 4.3 A chatbot avatar

Can we use any kind of programming language for AI?

Researchers wanted to be able to write programs that represented and manipulated knowledge. Ordinary **procedural** or **event-driven** languages, like Pascal or Visual Basic, often lacked the facilities to allow them to create AI programs. Researchers needed a different approach to programming which could represent knowledge. To meet this need **declarative** languages were devised.

The language **Prolog**, meaning '**pro**gramming in **log**ic', is probably the most common declarative language. It allowed programmers to write down facts and rules to describe a problem domain in full. Users could then solve problems by writing queries.

Facts are things we know, rules are relationships between facts. Some examples are:

English	Prolog
John is male	male(john).
Ruth likes jigsaws.	likes(ruth,jigsaws).
A cat is a mammal.	is_a(cat,mammal).
A cat has four legs.	legs(cat,4).
Iain was born in June.	birthmonth(iain,june).
Bob likes females who like snooker.	likes(bob,X) :- female(X),likes(X,snooker).

Another example of this type of language is **LISP**. However, the Intermediate 2 course concentrates on Prolog-type syntax, so LISP is only mentioned here for completeness. More detail on the Prolog language can be found in the last section of this chapter.

Chapter 4

Applications and uses of artificial intelligence

Expert systems

The creation of knowledge representation languages that allowed the manipulation of lists of facts and rules led directly to the development of **expert systems**. This kind of system takes in a query from the user and uses **pattern matching** to compare the query to the list of facts and rules, called the **knowledge base**. It can then give advice or solutions to problems within its problem domain.

To create an expert system you need one or more experts in a given field, called **domain experts**. You decide on the boundaries or limitations of the system and then get the expert(s) to write down or describe everything they know about the topic. You might also consult textbooks or manuals on the topic. This phase is called **knowledge acquisition**. You then get a specialist programmer, called a **knowledge engineer**, to structure the knowledge and create a knowledge base of facts and rules. The knowledge engineer might also have to create the user interface and the engine that solves the problems.

There are several advantages of expert systems over human experts. These include:

- The expertise is always available, 24 hours a day.
- Once purchased there is no need to pay wages to an expert.
- The system may combine the expertise of several experts.
- There is less chance of an error, as the system cannot forget or ignore something.
- Unlike human experts, expert systems cannot leave the company and take their knowledge with them.

However, many people are quite sceptical about advice given by a computer, and human experts are capable of making logical jumps or guesses, generally beyond a computer.

Below is a table showing some contemporary applications of expert systems.

Area/topic	Name of expert system	Description
Medical/chemical	MYCIN (1979)	Medical system for diagnosing blood disorders.
	PUFF (1983)	Medical system for diagnosing respiratory disorders.
	DENDRAL (1965)	One of the first expert systems, used for identifying chemical compounds.
Geology	PROSPECTOR	Used by geologists to identify likely sites for drilling/mining.
Computing	X-CON (1980s)	Used to help set up DEC computer networks.
	Design Advisor	Used to give advice on design of new processors.
Law and order	AFIS	Automated Fingerprint Identification System.
	SHYSTER	Used to give legal advice in Australia.

Area/topic	Name of expert system	Description
Financial	ExperTax, LoanProbe, ASQ, FSA	Used to give advice on tax returns, assess loans, audit accounts and do quality reviews.
Agriculture	LIMEX, CITEX	Used in Egypt to give advice to farmers.
Governmental	XpertRule	Used by New Zealand Social Welfare Department to assess eligibility for State benefits.

There are legal and ethical issues surrounding the use of expert systems. Medical expert systems are now very advanced and are used to support doctors, helping them to come to a diagnosis. The NHS website even has one to give advice to patients online.

Would you be happy to accept medical advice that is given by a computer program? Should you rely on it? Also, if the advice turns out to be wrong, who accepts legal responsibility for any consequences? Should the ultimate responsibility rest with:

- The patient who followed the advice?
- The doctor who gave the advice?
- The company who sold the software?
- The programmer who wrote the program code?
- The expert who provided the specialist knowledge about the topic?

To avoid such problems, most of these systems come with a disclaimer stating that the advice is to be followed at the user's own risk. As before, the final advice comes from the doctor and the final decision is in the hands of the patient.

The social issues involved in the introduction of expert systems include the potential loss of jobs, particularly the reduced need for experts. This shift away from human experts will reduce the number of experts in a given field. There are also training issues, both in the use of expert systems and in how to construct them. There is also a possible shift in the public's reaction to the experts themselves. If they can get the same advice from a machine, will they place the same value on the expertise of the human professionals?

Artificial neural systems (ANS)

Artificial neural systems, or **neural nets**, can be thought of as an electronic model of the brain. Just as the brain is made up of a large number of interconnected **neurons**, the neural net is made up of many interconnected simple processors. These are either implemented as physical circuits or as a piece of software. Neural nets do not follow a set algorithm or path of execution like a conventional program, but recognise patterns in data.

You have to **train** a neural net to get the correct answers to known problems, adjusting the connections to get the answers to match. Once this is done for all the known inputs and outputs, the network is fixed. The neural net is then given real input data, for which the answer is not known

Figure 4.4

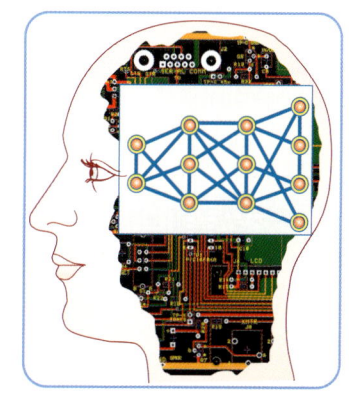

and the system will evaluate which of the possible outputs is most likely. Neural nets are very good at problems involving **pattern recognition**.

Neural nets have many applications in industry and elsewhere. The Post Office uses neural nets to automate the reading of postcodes. This is done by the net reacting to the individual characteristics of a letter, curves and crosses, and the most likely choice of character being made.

Financial institutions program neural nets to react to very small changes in share buying patterns and use these to predict changes in the stock market. Neural nets are also used to give advice on granting loans to customers.

Meteorologists also track small changes in temperature and air pressure. They then compare this to historical data, looking for patterns. Neural nets are good at spotting these patterns and therefore improving our chances of predicting the weather.

In fact, any pattern recognition task, such as software helping the police to identify fingerprints or faces, is ideally suited to being implemented using a neural network, as it picks up on small similarities and alerts the user when there is enough to make a match.

Advantages and disadvantages of ANS

Other than the standard advantages of any AI program, the advantages in the use of neural nets are their ability to process very complex problems and to spot links which are not obvious.

The main disadvantage is that they are very expensive to set up. Whether the neural networks are built as complex electronic circuits or written as complex programs, their creation is time consuming and requires a high degree of expertise.

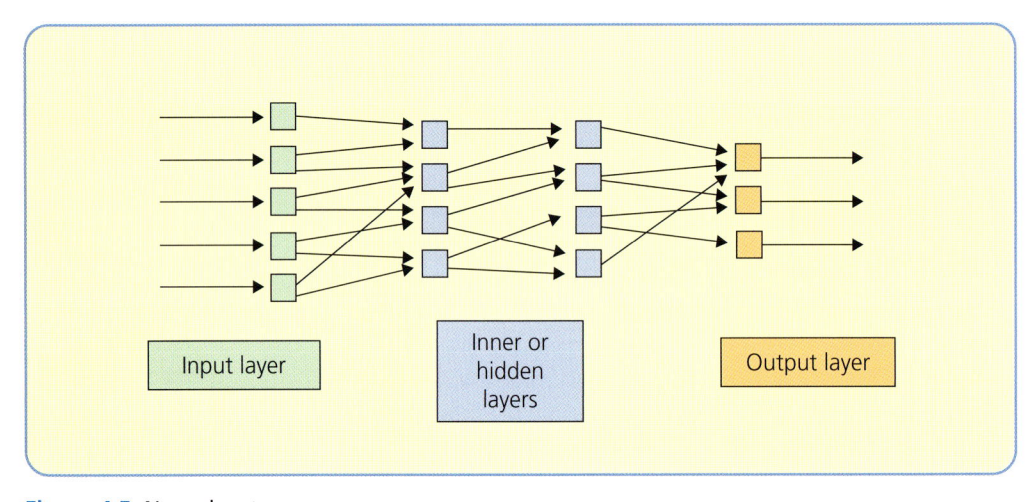

Figure 4.5 Neural net

Questions

Q1 Describe two features of human intelligence that AI is trying to mimic.

Q2 Describe how the Turing test is used.

Q3 Describe the role of the knowledge engineer and domain expert in creating an expert system.

Q4 Name an early example of language processing.

Q5 State two advantages of expert systems over human experts.

Q6 Describe one practical use of an artificial neural system.

Vision systems

Artificial Intelligence is used in vision systems to help interpret, or make sense of, visual input. This can be very tricky, even for humans! For example, in Figure 4.6 are you looking down on six cubes stacked together or up at seven?

There are many applications of vision systems. They are used heavily in modern industrial processing and manufacturing. For example, a camera looks down at a number of components and the robot recognises the processor chip, picks it up with its suction cup and spins it so that the clipped corner is at the right place before inserting it into the correct place on the motherboard.

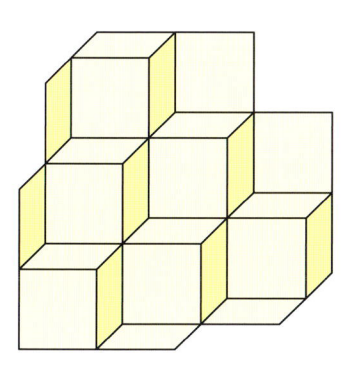

Figure 4.6 How many cubes?

Vision systems are also used by the military and security services. They are used in automatic face recognition so that images from airport security cameras can be automatically searched for faces of known criminals and terrorist suspects. The software notes key measurements like the distance between the eyes, the length of the nose etc. It then compares them to see if their ratios match any on file. You can wear a wig, but you cannot change the shape of your head very easily!

Vision systems are also used to distinguish between potential targets and friendly units in some missile and bomb guidance systems. Here the weapon is fired or dropped into a battle situation and it will automatically pick a target and home in on it.

A more constructive use of vision systems is the satellite photo interpretation system used to analyse the weather photographs taken by NASA and other agencies. These can

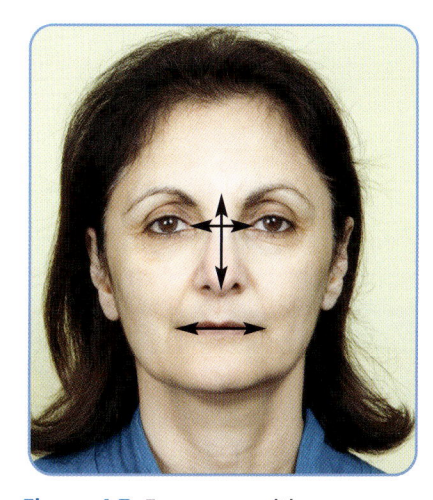

Figure 4.7 Face recognition

Chapter 4

give early warning of potential meteorological problems – that's very bad weather to you and me!

Speech recognition

Speech recognition systems are in use in a wide area of applications from speech to text programs, like DragonTalk or SimplySpeaking, to voice-activated controllers for a whole range of devices. You may have a mobile phone that will dial for you if you just tell it to 'Call Morag'. These are very useful tools for anyone, but just imagine the benefits that systems like these can bring to disabled users.

Before you can use this kind of device, it has to learn your voice. Each voice has a number of characteristics. Male voices are deeper, for instance. To train the software the user will have to speak a number of sentences designed to cover all the possible sounds. It is best to say these in an even tone, at the same volume and without small pauses between each of the words (which just confuses the software).

In 2006, a leading mobile phone company developed new voice recognition software. However, the whole development team was male and they had not trained it on female voices. The result of this was that it did not respond properly to the sound of a female trying to use it – a financial disaster was only narrowly avoided.

Even after the command words are programmed in and the software has been trained in a variety of voices it is not all plain sailing. Voices change for a number of reasons: regional accents, heavy colds, even just tiredness! The software must be able to cope with background noise, like traffic or another person speaking next to you.

Correctly trained, voice recognition software can be used to take dictation or control machinery. These systems are combined with chatterbots to answer queries, or direct you to someone who can, on telephone help lines.

Handwriting recognition

Another growing area of recognition software is handwriting recognition. Most tablet PCs and palmtop computers, or PDAs, have the facility to write notes using a stylus on their touch-sensitive screen. The software then converts these scribbles into editable text, just the same way as OCR software does.

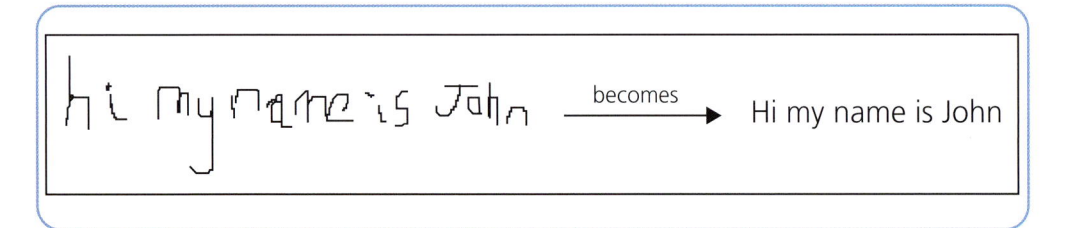

hi my name is John becomes → Hi my name is John

Figure 4.8

As you can tell with the above example, you might need to spend a little bit of time training the system. This would be done by prompting the user to write a specially selected set of words on the PDA screen. This allows the system to learn the letter shapes used by that particular person when they write. The system will have quite a few starting templates of the alphabet to start with, but that is often not enough to decode some people's handwriting.

Chapter 4

Intelligent robots

Robots are mechanical devices carrying out tasks we choose not to, or cannot, do for ourselves. They may be stationary, like robot arms in factories, or mobile, like remote submarines or even lawnmowers.

The main difference between a **dumb robot** and an **intelligent robot** is the presence of some form of AI. It might be very limited but it must have the ability to make choices or decisions or to learn.

In order to make a decision about the outside world, a robot needs to have data about that world. This data will be gathered using **sensors** – just like we use our eyes, ears, etc. There are various types of sensors, and robots are not limited in the same ways as humans.

There are sensors for detecting many things, including but not limited to:

- touch (bump switches)
- proximity (motion)
- pressure/weight
- magnetic fields
- sound
- light
- smell/smoke
- temperature
- air pressure
- altitude
- radioactivity
- humidity

It would be impossible to describe every example of the use of intelligent robots, but the four mentioned explicitly in the exam arrangements are: automated delivery, pipe inspection, bomb disposal and exploration of unknown environments.

Automated delivery robot

This is typically an automated cart running around a factory carrying parts or messages. It follows a painted line using light sensors or a wire in the floor using magnetic sensors to get around. It travels between the warehouse and various parts of the factory without any intervention by human workers. Similar robotic systems for you to look up on the Internet include lawnmowers, vacuum cleaners, pool cleaners and sentry robots.

Figure 4.9 An automated delivery robot

Pipe inspection robot

Pipe inspection robots are small tracked or wheeled robots that are put down pipes to look for welding flaws, structural cracking, blockages or other problems. They might use cameras, ultrasound or X-rays to help them get a picture. They might even be able to weld a leaking joint. There is current medical research into making very small versions of these to be injected into the bloodstream to locate and fix circulation or heart problems.

Figure 4.10 A bomb-disposal robot

ARTIFICIAL INTELLIGENCE

Chapter 4

Bomb-disposal robot
The military use a mobile robot, called the wheelbarrow, to help bomb-disposal squads. It carries sensors, cameras and other equipment and has a multi-jointed arm to help it locate bombs without danger to military personnel. A similar robot was used in Afghanistan to explore caves used by hostile forces to reduce risk to humans from ambush or booby traps.

Exploration robot
Exploration robots have been sent into space, even landing on Mars, and to the bottom of the deepest seas. They can be used for surveillance, e.g. the MSSMP system used by the military, or for mundane tasks like delivering mail around a building. Industry uses robots to manufacture goods. There is even a robotic fish swimming around helping us study the sea. Try looking up 'robotuna' on Google.

Advantages of robots
Robots can go where we cannot and 'see' things which are invisible to us. Robots can work tirelessly all day; they can be more accurate than humans in many tasks; robots are consistent in that they do the task over and over in exactly the same way; robots do not need to be paid. The advantages go on and on. There are very few jobs that cannot be automated to some extent, but are we ready for that?

Search techniques

Construction of a simple search tree

Most problems can be broken down into a series of simple steps leading from the start to the solution. Where there are a number of possible options the problem starts to look like a **tree**. The start of the problem, called the **initial state**, is at the top of the tree.

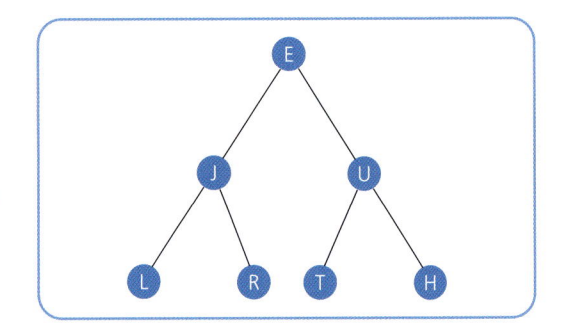

Figure 4.11 Simple search tree

In the example shown here in Figure 4.11 the problem starts at point E. In the first move the system can move to point J or point U. If the system moves to J it then has the choice of moving to point L or point R. One of these points will be the solution to our problem, called the **goal state**.

Example

Example of problem-solving by search

Using a simple game as an example we will explore how an AI system builds a search tree of all possible states.

The game starts with three piles of matches, as shown. The idea is to

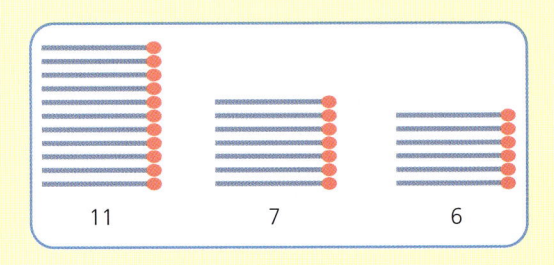

11   7   6

Figure 4.12

Example continued ➤

Example continued

move matches from one pile to another so that each pile ends up with eight matches in it. The only problem is that you are only allowed to move matches to double the number already in the pile and you cannot leave a pile with no matches in it.

The search tree looks something like this:

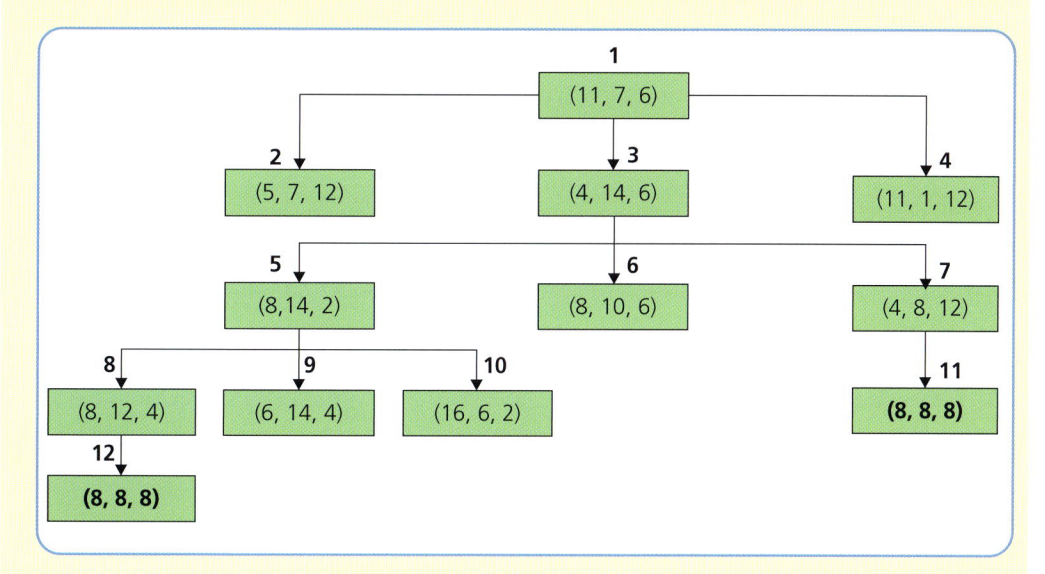

```
                        1
                    (11, 7, 6)
        ┌───────────────┼───────────────┐
        2               3               4
    (5, 7, 12)      (4, 14, 6)     (11, 1, 12)
        │               │               │
        5               6               7
    (8, 14, 2)      (8, 10, 6)      (4, 8, 12)
   ┌────┼────┐                          │
   8    9    10                         11
(8,12,4)(6,14,4)(16,6,2)             (8, 8, 8)
   │
   12
(8, 8, 8)
```

Figure 4.13

What You Should Know

About breadth-first and depth-first searches

There are two techniques for searching the tree shown here. The first of these is **breadth-first**. In this technique the system begins at the start state (point A) and looks at each state that is one move away (points B and C).

If the system has not found the goal state, it will move on to the states that are two moves away. It looks at each of these in turn, running from left to right.

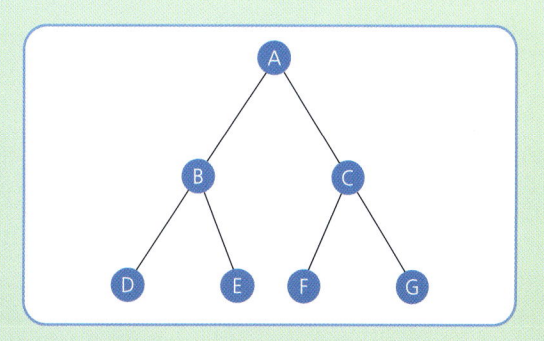

Figure 4.14

What you should know continued

71

Chapter 4

> **What You Should Know** continued
>
> The search goes all the way across the tree before moving down to the next level. The order that the states are visited in a breadth-first search is **ABCDEFG**.
>
> The other technique is called **depth-first**. Here the search starts at the start state (point A) and then makes the first available move (point B). If it does not find a solution there it tries the next state along that search path (point D). If it does not find a solution here, and there are no more moves from that state, it will **backtrack** to the last time it had a choice and try the other path.
>
> The search follows one path, or branch, all the way to the end before backtracking to try the next branch. The order that the states are visited in a depth-first search is **ABDECFG**.
>
> For the matches problem above, using the numbers, the order of searching is as follows:
> - The path followed by a breadth-first search is 1, 2, 3, 4, 5, 6, 7, 8, 9, 10, 11. So a goal state is found after 11 states have been checked. The goal state found is only three moves away from the start state.
> - The path followed by a depth-first search is 1, 2, 3, 5, 8, 12. So a goal state is found after six states have been checked. The goal state is only four moves away from the start state.

Knowledge representation

Before we can manipulate knowledge, we have to find a way to write it down in a form that both we and the computer can understand. There are two ways to do this in this course. Knowledge can be represented by a list of facts and rules in a **declarative** or **knowledge representation language**, like PROLOG. It can also be represented graphically in a diagram called a **semantic net**.

> **Key Points**
>
> ### Semantic net
>
> A semantic net is just a diagram showing how a group of things relate to each other.
>
> Constructing a semantic net of a group of facts and relationships is a relatively easy task.
>
> Figure 4.15 is a semantic net containing information about part of a family.
>
> *Key Points continued >*

Key Points continued

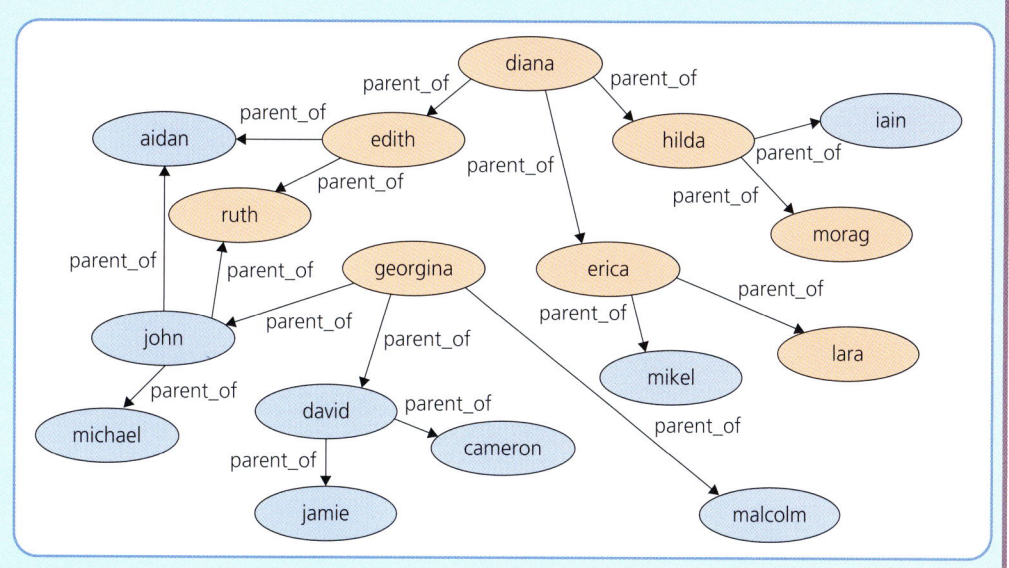

Figure 4.15 Semantic net

This diagram is useful, as you can trace all of the relationships in the family. However, if we were to try to include all of the relatives, the diagram would get very large and very complex quite quickly. Such diagrams are extremely useful when modelling some of the data for a new system and trying to get the overall structure correct. You can get software that will allow you to create a semantic net and then generate the code automatically.

Knowledge representation language

Declarative or knowledge representation languages, like Prolog, allow us to write down **facts** and **rules** in a formal way. Rules are **relationships** between facts. This allows us to write **queries**, formal questions for the knowledge base, which the system will try to match. The thing we are looking for is called the **goal**. Any problems that need to be solved on the way to the goal are called **subgoals**, sometimes written as **sub-goals**.

Key Points

Facts

Facts can be simple or more complex. Here are some facts about books:

```
male(john).              author(john,htp_higher_computing).
male(frank).             author(frank,htp_int2_computing).
```

Key Points continued ➤

Chapter 4

Key Points continued

```
male(terry).                author(frank,htp_sgrade_computing).
book(htp_int2_computing).   author(terry,wintersmith).
book(mort).                author(terry,mort).
```

The first three facts have a single **argument**, the thing in the brackets. The last two have two arguments each. Note the lack of capital letters. Prolog uses capitals for variables, so it does not use them anywhere else. The proper name for a fact here is a **predicate** but don't worry about it. You can read these facts as 'There is a male called John', 'There is a book called Mort', 'Terry is the author of Mort'. If we were to write a simple query to find the name of a book that Frank has written it would look like this:

```
?author(frank,Book).
```

Key Points

Variables

Here the variable called 'Book' is used to stand in for the thing we want to find out about. A variable **must** start with a capital letter. It could have been called X, or A, or any other single capital, but that is not as readable. The SQA exam that you will sit will probably use a single capital letter for a variable. The system starts at the top of the knowledge base and looks for a fact called 'author' with two arguments, the first one being 'frank'. It will find a fact that matches what it is looking for and it will display an answer for 'Book' like this:

```
Book = htp_int2_computing;
```

Using a knowledge representation language

Using the information from the family semantic net in Figure 4.15, a set of facts can be written down. Facts about gender have been added to the knowledge in the semantic net.

```
male(john).             parent(john,ruth).
male(david).            parent(john,aidan).
male(aidan).            parent(john,michael).
male(michael).          parent(edith,ruth).
male(jamie).            parent(edith,aidan).
male(cameron).          parent(edith,michael).
male(iain).             parent(georgina,john).
male(mikel).            parent(georgina,david).
male(malcolm).          parent(georgina,malcolm).
female(edith).          parent(hilda,morag).
female(ruth).           parent(hilda,iain).
female(hilda).          parent(erica,lara).
```

```
female(morag).              parent(erica,mikel).
female(georgina).           parent(david,jamie).
female(diana).              parent(david,cameron).
female(erica).              parent(diana,erica).
female(lara).               parent(diana,hilda).
                            parent(diana,edith).
```

There is a male( ) or a female( ) fact for every object in the semantic net and there is a parent( ) fact, with two arguments, for every line in the semantic net.

Here are a few queries with their answers.

Query	Response
? female(morag)	yes
? parent(hilda,iain)	yes
? parent(X,edith)	X = diana
? parent(david,Child)	Child = jamie, Child = cameron

The first two queries get the output 'yes' (some systems use the word 'true'). This is because it has found a fact matching the query. The third query is compared to each of the 'parent' facts looking for an instance where 'edith' appears, looking for a value for the empty variable. The technical name for finding this value is **instantiation**, but don't worry about that. The fourth query has two solutions.

Key Points

Rules

As we have seen, facts are things that the system knows are true. **Rules** are ways of combining facts. Using the family database to create a simple rule:

```
mother(A,B) :- parent(A,B) , female(A).
```

This rule means 'A is the mother of B **IF** A is the parent of B **AND** A is female'.

Example

To see how this would work we are going to find out if Edith is Ruth's mother using the following query:

```
? mother(edith,ruth).
```

The **goal** of the rule is 'mother(edith,ruth)'. This is only **true** if both of the **subgoals**, 'parent(edith,ruth)' and 'female(edith)' are **true**. The system will look at each of the subgoals in turn and evaluate them. If the first is true it will then check the second one. If the first subgoal is not true, then the goal cannot be true and the query would return 'false' or 'no'. Here are a few queries about mothers with their answers.

Key Points continued ➢

Chapter 4

Key Points continued

Query	Response
? mother(erica,mikel)	yes
? mother(john,ruth)	no
? mother(X,malcolm)	X = georgina
? mother(hilda,Child)	Child = morag, Child = iain

It is possible to create quite a lot of rules to help define relationships in the knowledge base. Here are a couple more…

```
father(Adult,Child) :- parent(Adult,Child) , male(Adult).
son(Child,Adult) :- parent(Adult,Child) , male(Child).
```

The first of these rules is read as: 'Adult is the father of Child **IF** Adult is the parent of Child **AND** Adult is male'. Each of the two subgoals must be true for the goal to succeed.

Comparison operators

For this course you have to be able to use comparison operators. These are greater than, less than and equals. We will now explore this using a knowledge base about girls and fairground rides:

1. height(mary,156).
2. height(kerry,172).
3. height(sophina,147).
4. height(katie,161).
5. height(susan,159).
6. height(kirsty,167).
7. height(alex,158).
8. height(mia,176).
9. height(debbie,174).
10. height(ruth,106).
11. limit(thunderclap,170).
12. limit(whirlwind,160).
13. limit(astrodrop,150).
14. limit(teacups,100).
15. can_ride(Person,Ride) :- height(Person,H), limit(Ride,L), H > L.

The solution to the query:

? can-ride(ruth,whirlwind).

is **no**.

This is because the first subgoal finds **H = 106**, the second subgoal finds **L = 160**, but the third subgoal **fails** as 106 is **not** greater than 160. Alas four-year-old Ruth is **still** too short this year!

Tracing a solution

When the system finds a solution it follows a path through the knowledge base using pattern matching. You are expected to explain how a query is solved by tracing the solution. The knowledge base we are going to use for the next few examples is shown below. It has line numbers to help explain when doing a trace.

1. male(john).
2. male(aidan).
3. female(edith).
4. female(ruth).
5. female(diana).
6. female(georgina).
7. parent(john,ruth).
8. parent(edith,ruth).
9. parent(john,aidan).
10. parent(edith,aidan).
11. parent(diana,edith).
12. parent(georgina,john).
13. mother(A,B) :- parent(A,B) , female(A).
14. father(A,B) :- parent(A,B) , male(A).
15. grandmother(Gran,Child) :- parent(Gran,P) , parent(P,Child),female(Gran).

Example

Trace the solution to the query: ? mother(Mum,ruth).
- Goal is mother(Mum,ruth).
- Match at line 15, first subgoal is parent(Mum,ruth).
- Match at line 7, Mum = john, second subgoal is female(john).
- Fails to match, backtrack to find another parent of ruth.
- Match at line 8, Mum = edith, second subgoal is female(edith).
- Match at line 3, subgoal succeeds.
- Goal succeeds, display Mum = edith.

Chapter 4

You are going to get a trace in your exam, so you need to practise them until you have the format down perfectly.

Questions

Q7 State two problems that a vision system on a robot truck would have to overcome.

Q8 In the future, mobile phones may not have a keypad. Name an area of artificial intelligence that will allow the user to enter a phone number and describe how this will work.

Q9 Give two advantages of an intelligent robot compared to a robot with no intelligence.

Q10 Describe how Frank's computer is able to interpret his spoken commands.

Q11 Describe two factors affecting the accuracy of speech recognition.

Q12 How does Jonny train his palmtop computer to understand his handwriting?

Q13 Explain the meanings of the terms 'goal', 'subgoal' and 'trace'.

Q14 Describe two of the sensors that a mine rescue robot might have.

Q15 State two advances in computer hardware that have supported the development of artificial intelligence applications.

Q16 State one early computer game that demonstrates artificial intelligence.

Q17 Use letters to show the order in which the nodes in the tree shown here (Figure 4.16) are visited using a depth-first search and a breadth-first search.

Q18 Construct facts from the semantic net on page 79 (Figure 4.17).

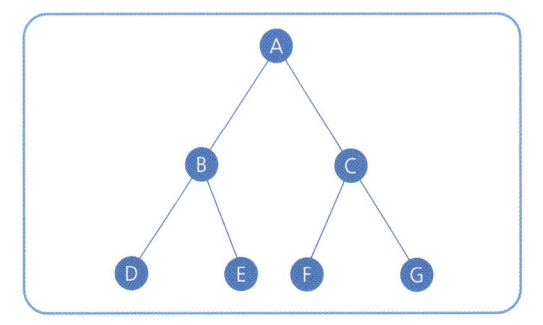

Figure 4.16

Questions continued ➢

Questions continued

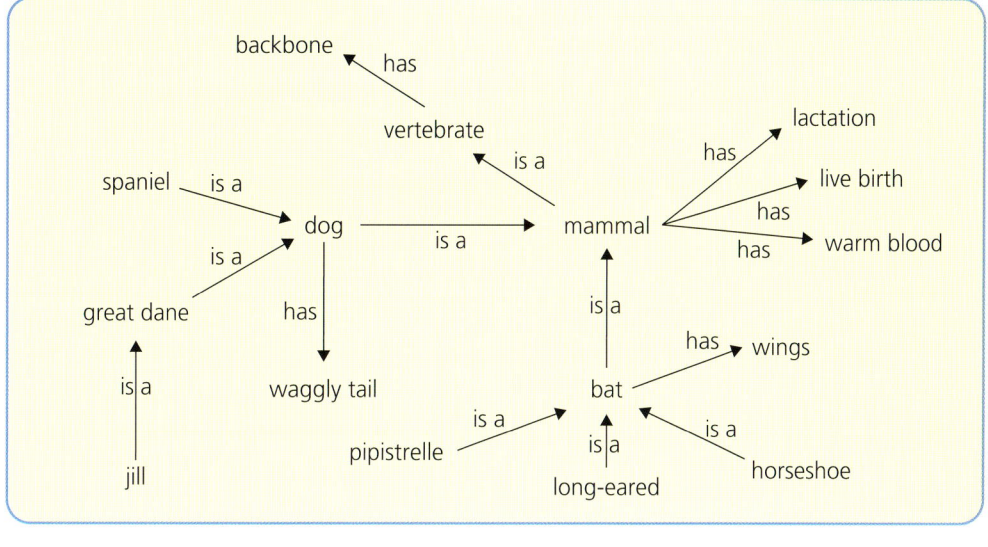

Figure 4.17

A semantic network showing:
- spaniel **is a** dog
- great dane **is a** dog
- jill **is a** great dane
- dog **is a** mammal
- dog **has** waggly tail
- dog **is a** vertebrate
- vertebrate **has** backbone
- mammal **has** lactation
- mammal **has** live birth
- mammal **has** warm blood
- bat **is a** mammal
- bat **has** wings
- pipistrelle **is a** bat
- long-eared **is a** bat
- horseshoe **is a** bat

Chapter 5

MULTIMEDIA TECHNOLOGY

Developing a multimedia application

There are seven stages involved in developing a multimedia application.

Analysis

Analysis turns a vague idea into an exact description of what the multimedia project is expected to do.

Design

Design produces a detailed plan which defines what the different parts of the project are and how they are linked together. It contains important details about the content of the project, the number and type of graphics required, and the need for sound files and video clips. The best way to do all of this is to make a **storyboard**.

Implementation

The multimedia authoring, or web-page authoring, package is used to turn the design into a working project combining the graphics, the video clips, the text files and the sound files.

Testing

A series of practical tests are carried out to check that the multimedia project functions properly.

Documentation

A user guide is produced containing advice to help people use the finished project.

A technical guide is produced containing information about the specification of the computer system and software required to run the project.

Evaluation

Evaluation checks ensure that the finished application meets the user's requirements.

Maintenance

Maintenance involves fixing bugs and adapting the design to suit client needs and the demands of new technology.

Chapter 5

MULTIMEDIA TECHNOLOGY

What You Should Know

About implementing a multimedia project

You can create multimedia web pages using a **text editor** to produce HTML code.

Use applications that let you see exactly what the finished page will look like: they usually have a preview facility. This is called **WYSIWYG** – what you see is what you get.

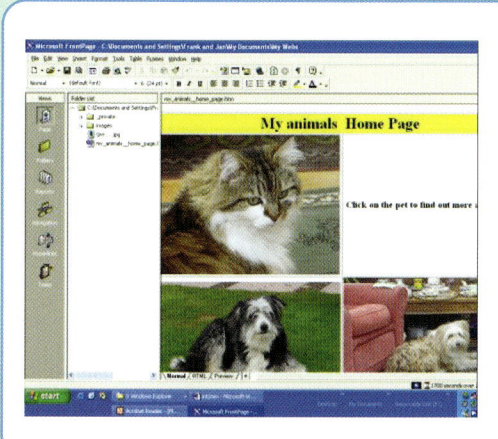

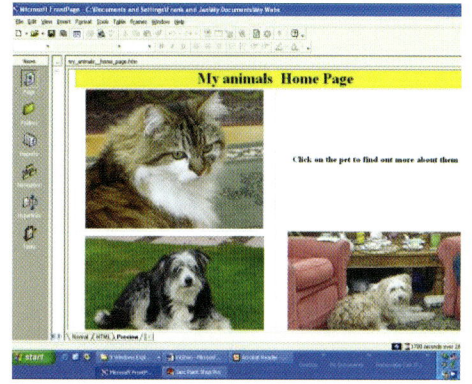

Figure 5.1 A web page under construction   The same page being previewed

There are many **authoring packages** designed to help you implement a multimedia project. Try an Internet search to get a list.

You can use **presentation software** such as Powerpoint.

To **display** a multimedia application you need either a browser like Explorer, Firefox or Chrome or a file player or viewer.

Figure 5.2

Using multimedia authoring software means that you can save a project as an **executable file** which can run on its own without a player or viewer.

81

Chapter 5

Key Points

Capturing bit-mapped graphic data

Capturing still images using a digital camera

Digital cameras use an electronic circuit called a charged coupled device, **CCD**, to capture light coming in through a lens. A CCD has sensors which capture the light coming in through the lens and change it into digital data.

Storing the images in the camera
The digital images are then stored on a form of removable backing storage called flash memory, sometimes called a memory stick, memory card or flash card.

Figure 5.3 A memory stick

Capturing images using a scanner

Scanners have CCD in a movable scan head. This passes over a document converting the light reflected off the document into an analogue signal which is then converted to digital data and stored in the computer system attached to the scanner.

Key Points

Compressing graphics

An uncompressed bitmap graphic file contains data about each pixel that makes up the image. In a bitmap file of a simple black and white image each pixel would be represented by a single bit set to '1' or '0'.

Uncompressed bitmap graphics:
- can be very large
- take up lots of storage space
- take longer to transmit across networks.

Compressing the graphics makes the file size smaller.

Compressing graphics using GIF

- The GIF file format uses **lossless compression** to reduce the file size without losing any of the data about the image. It does this by using a code to store patterns of bits that occur repeatedly throughout a graphic file.

Key Points continued ➤

Key Points *continued*

- GIF is based on an 8-bit colour code giving a maximum of 2^8, or 256, colours. A maximum of 256 colours means that GIFs are unsuitable for storing photographic images and are used to represent charts, cartoons, or drawings.

Compressing graphics using JPEG

- The JPEG file format is a bitmap graphics file format which uses **lossy compression**. This makes the graphic file smaller by cutting out parts of the graphic that won't be noticed by the human eye.
- It is often used when storing digital photographs.
- JPEG is not used for storing cartoons or drawings because some of the data is lost and this reduces the quality of the image.

Key Points

Trading quality for file size

When processing graphic data we can choose to vary the **resolution**, the **colour depth** as well as use different levels of **lossy compression**. Involved in using each of these is a trade off between file size and image quality.

Increasing levels of compression

JPEG files can vary in their level of compression. The higher the level of compression, the smaller the file size. The smaller the file size, the more data is lost and the poorer the quality of the graphic.

Changing the resolution

The resolution is the number of pixels used to represent a graphic e.g. 300 × 300 pixels per inch. Increasing the resolution increases the size of the file and produces a higher quality graphic.

Increasing the colour depth

The colour depth is the number of bits used to represent the colour of each pixel in a graphic. As the colour depth increases so does the size of the file.

Colour depth	Number of possible colours per pixel	File size for a bitmap 3 inches × 3 inches at a resolution of 600 pixels per inch
1 bit	2, black or white	405000 bytes = 395.5 kilobytes
8 bit	256 colours	3240000 bytes = 3.08 megabytes

Chapter 5

Questions

Q1 Arrange the seven stages of the software development cycle below into the correct order:

maintenance testing analysis implementation design documentation evaluation

Q2 What software do you need to see a multimedia project?

Q3 How does a digital camera capture images?

Q4 What does compression do to the file size of an image?

Q5 What is lossless compression? Give an example.

Q6 What is lossy compression? Give an example.

Q7 How many colours can there be in a GIF graphic?

Q8 What is the effect of changing the colour depth of a graphic from 8 bits to 24 bits per pixel?

Q9 State two effects of increasing the resolution of a graphic.

Paint programs and image editing software

Paint programs

Paint programs let you make changes to bitmap images. Two common tools are the **Fill Tool**, which lets you choose colour from a chart and then pour it into the graphic, and the **Paintbrush Tool**, which lets you apply colour in a more controlled way to parts of the graphic.

Image editing software

Once a graphic has been loaded into the editing software (for example, from a digital camera) the software can be used to:

- **Alter the resolution** – the lower the resolution, the smaller the number of pixels, the poorer the quality of hard copy, the smaller the file size.
- **Alter colour depth** – increasing the colour depth increases both the quality of a graphic and its file size.
- **Crop** – select parts of a graphic and cut out what is not needed.
- **Alter brightness and contrast** to lighten up shady areas and improve the overall appearance of the image.
- **Re-size or scale** to adjust the width and/or height of a graphic.
- **Use special effects** – image editing packages have a whole range of special effects which can be used to enhance a graphic.

Chapter 5

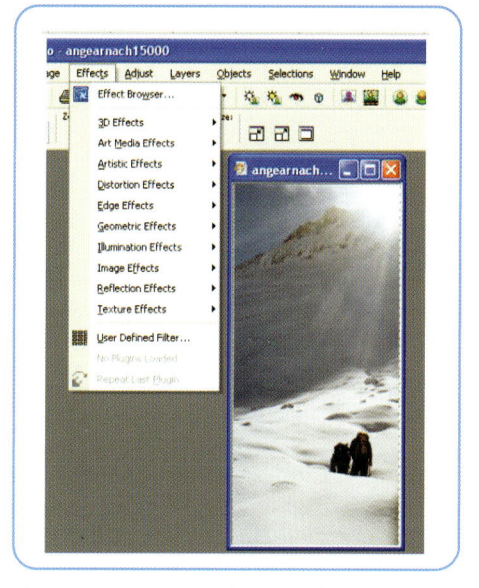

MULTIMEDIA TECHNOLOGY

Figure 5.4 Image editing software (Paint Shop Pro)
© Corel Corporation

Hardware for displaying graphics

Key Points

CRT monitors

- CRT (cathode ray tube) monitors are large and very heavy.
- Medium and high resolution monitors display very high quality images.
- High resolution displays are more effective on monitors with larger screen sizes, between e.g. 17 and 21 inches.
- High resolution monitors are needed for CAD work and art work.

Note: the higher the screen resolution the more pixels on the screen, the clearer the image. See below for a table showing the resolution of different standards of monitors.

Mode	Resolution
SVGA	800 × 600
SXGA	1280 × 1024
UXGA	1600 × 1200
QWXGA	2048 × 1152

85

Chapter 5

Key Points

LCD and TFT screens

Liquid crystal display (LCD)

LCD screens use transistors and a thin film of liquid crystals to control the light passing through the screen. They are often found on palmtop and laptop computers because they are light, compact, need little power and can be run on batteries. One problem is that some LCD screens are not very bright and can cause eye strain if they are used for too long.

Thin film transistor (TFT)

TFT is a type of LCD screen that uses lots of transistors to produce a high quality display. A TFT screen can display animations and 3-D graphics much more clearly than ordinary LCD screens. The disadvantage is that TFT screens can be a lot more expensive than ordinary LCD screens.

On desktop computers TFT screens are used because they take up less space on a desk than CRT monitors and are less awkward to move around.

Key Points

Graphics Cards

Graphics cards have their own on-board memory and processor which are used to relieve the pressure on the computer's main processor and memory. This is because processing the graphics, animations and video clips in a multimedia project can take up lots of the processor's main memory.

Figure 5.5

Converging technologies

Converging technologies simply means two or more technologies being combined. You need to know about smart phones, Pocket PC and digital television.

Chapter 5

MULTIMEDIA TECHNOLOGY

Key Points

Smartphone

A smartphone:

- is a mobile phone with a memory to hold an address book and ring tones, and the ability to send, receive and store text messages etc.
- is a multimedia device which can handle text, graphics, audio and video
- has a browser to access web pages and send email
- has a digital camera to capture images and send them through the phone network and even the Internet
- can play MP3 files and games
- can connect with laptops and desktops.

Key Points

Pocket PC

This is a hand-held palmtop computer which has an operating system and applications normally available only on a desktop or a laptop. It has:

- 'Windows for Pocket PC' operating system
- compact versions of applications that run on windows: Pocket Office applications (Internet Explorer, Word and Excel)
- handwriting recognition and/or voice recognition capabilities
- a touch screen
- MP3 playback
- voice recording
- an e-book reader
- wireless Internet connection
- USB ports
- the ability to link up with desktops/laptops.

Key Points

Digital television, DTV

DTV is an interactive multimedia device which:

- is capable of displaying high quality audio, video, animation and text
- enables users to interact with the broadcast
- can link up to your computer or home network
- can be accessed over the Internet.

87

Chapter 5

Virtual reality

The ultimate multimedia experience

Virtual reality (VR) is the ultimate multimedia experience where the user is immersed in the world of the computer and can journey through, and interact with, a computer generated three-dimensional multimedia world.

What You Should Know

About VR

What VR is used for:

- training e.g. pilots
- creating and inspecting a 3-D CAD model
- simulating scientific processes such as the creation of molecular structures of chemical compounds
- gaming.

Several technologies are used to interact with a virtual reality world.

Input devices:

- data gloves fitted with fibre optic sensors to sense finger bending
- data suits equipped with multiple sensors.

Sensors:

- magnetic trackers
- ultrasonic tracking systems
- optical position sensors.

Video output

Video 3-D output can be achieved by using split-screen technology, multiple projectors or headsets equipped with miniature stereo monitors.

Audio output

This is achieved by sets of surround sound speakers either embedded in a headset or placed around a VR room.

Questions

Q10 How does a crop tool help you edit a graphic?

Q11 List three special effects that graphics editing software can have.

Q12 Describe two differences between an ordinary LCD monitor and a TFT monitor.

Questions continued ➢

Chapter 5

MULTIMEDIA TECHNOLOGY

Questions *continued*

Q13 Why does a graphics card have its own processor and on-board memory?

Q14 Explain why a smart phone is a good example of converging technology.

Q15 Why is virtual reality described as the ultimate multimedia experience?

Digitised sound data

An important component of any multimedia application is the inclusion of sound data. This might be a clip downloaded from the Internet, copied from a CD or it could be captured live. It might be spoken instructions for the user, a commentary running over the action or just some music or sound effects to make the application more interesting.

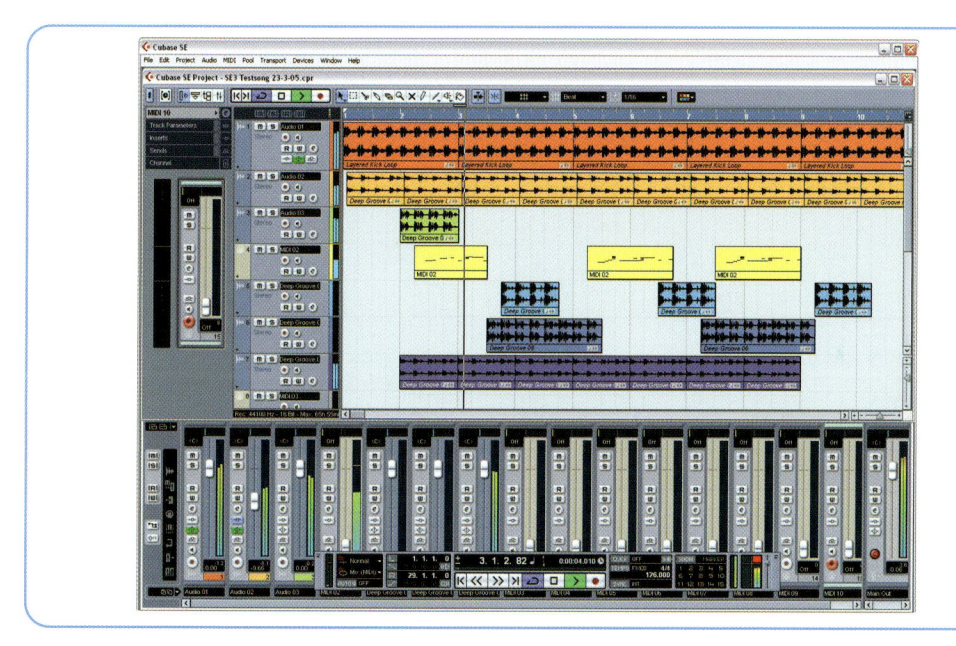

Figure 5.6

You might just want to edit, or add some effects to, a sound clip or piece of music. For this you will need a sound editing package.

If you are trying to capture a voice commentary or some live music, you need to make sure that you have the necessary hardware attached to, or installed in, your computer. You will need a **sound card** and **microphone**.

Figure 5.7

Chapter 5

Key Points

Sound cards

Sound cards contain processors and memory chips. They are installed in your computer and they take over some of the hard work of the processing of sound data. They can do a number of different things including:

- recording audio directly onto the hard disk
- playback of digitised sound
- playback of audio tracks from CDs and DVDs
- sound synthesis
- interfacing with MIDI instruments.

The sound card captures the sound as a wave. It then samples this wave as a series of numbers. These numbers are then converted to digital values and processed by the processor. The sound card also plays a vital role in the playback of audio, along with speakers.

Figure 5.8

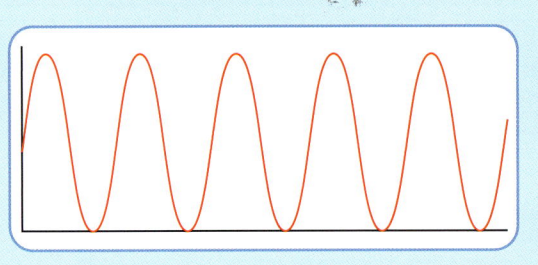

Figure 5.9 A sound wave

Key Points

Audio formats

Sound data can be stored in **compressed** and **uncompressed** formats. The advantage of an uncompressed format is that you get all of the data, so no information is lost from the original recording. However, uncompressed audio files tend to be huge.

You may be aware of a number of different audio formats. The most common ones are **RAW** (uncompressed audio data), **WAV** (the audio component of RIFF) and **MP3** (the audio layer of MPEG, layer 3). WAV and MP3 use compression.

Chapter 5

What You Should Know

About file size

There are a number of factors that can have an effect on the size of a sound file. Some of these are described below:

Lossy compression is used to reduce file size by removing some of the original data and leaving the quality of the sound largely unchanged. The MP3 format removes data that is outwith the normal hearing range. It also removes quieter sounds which would be drowned out by other parts of the recording. Compression of any sort reduces file size, but you may sacrifice some sound quality. Just think of the difference between CD-quality audio and an MP3 track.

Sampling depth, also called **sample resolution**, is the number of bits, or bytes, used to store a single sample. The greater the sample depth, the more detailed the digital picture of the original sound will be. However, a high sample depth could mean a very large file. Figure 5.10 shows a sound stored with a low sample depth; the sound wave on the right does not look much like the original sound on the left. If the blocks were to be made narrower we would get a picture that was much closer to the original wave. WAV files are sampled using a bit depth of 8 or 16 bits.

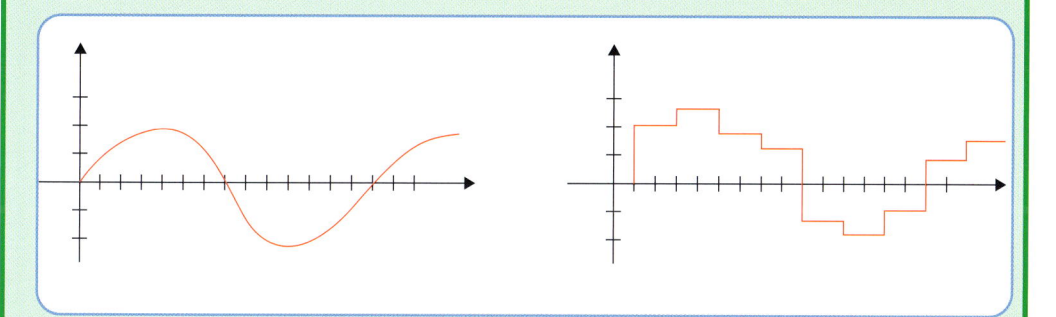

Figure 5.10 Original sound wave and stored sound wave

Sampling frequency is how often the sound is sampled in a second. It is measured in hertz (Hz) or, more usually, kilohertz (kHz). Standard sampling rates are 44.1 kHz, 22.05 kHz or 11.025 kHz. The more often you sample, the better the sound quality, but the file size is going to be larger as a result. It is a bit like the frame rate of a video: if you set it too low the playback is jerky.

Sound time is the duration of the clip in seconds. Obviously longer tracks take up more space.

MULTIMEDIA TECHNOLOGY

Chapter 5

Key Points

Sound editing software

The main features of simple sound editing software include the ability to:

- Decrease the sampling frequency to reduce file size at the loss of some sound quality.
- Decrease the resolution, or sampling depth, to make the sound file smaller – although the playback is of poorer quality, often sounding quite metallic.
- Crop the sound file, shortening the track or even removing parts of it. You can create an audio loop or grab a sample that can be used in another track.
- Apply a range of effects, such as adding echo/reverb or even reversing sections of the track so that it runs backwards.
- Adjust the volume of sections or tracks within the sample. By changing the volume of various instruments, you can mix your own track.

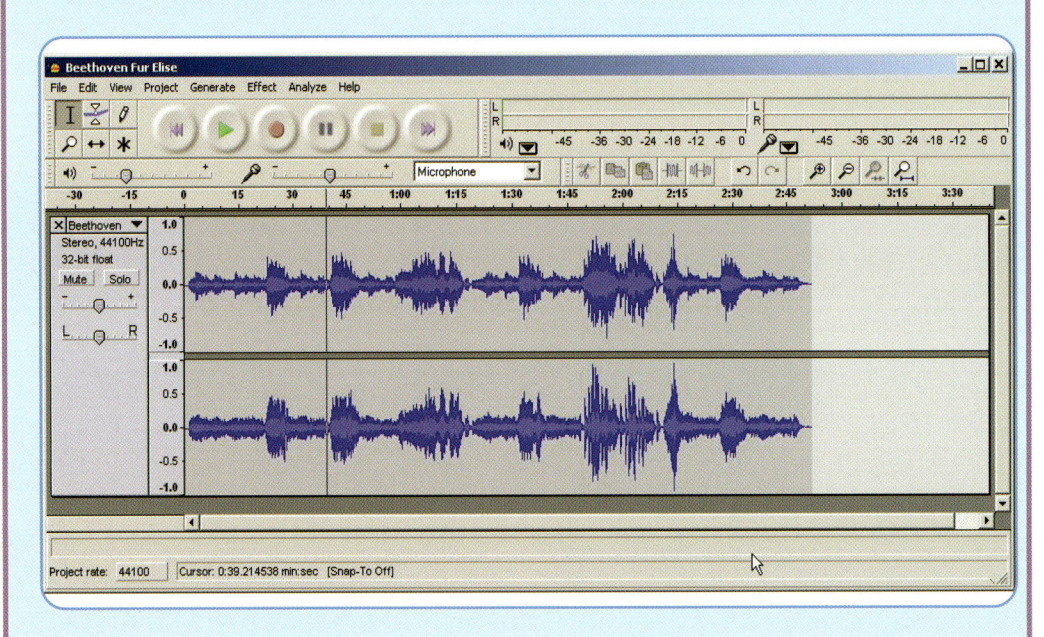

Figure 5.11

Key Points continued

Chapter 5

MULTIMEDIA TECHNOLOGY

Key Points continued

Figure 5.12

Synthesised sound data

Another way of producing music or sound, other than capturing actual sounds and storing them digitally, is to make the computer produce its own. This way of producing artificial sound is called **synthesising**.

Most music keyboards are now synthesisers. In order for each of these devices to be able to swap data with each other, or with the computer, they have to have a common format for storing the data. One of the most common formats is the **Musical Instrument Digital Interface**, or MIDI for short.

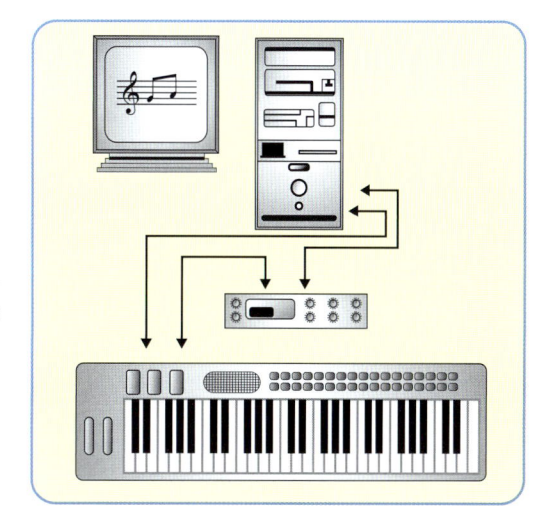

Figure 5.13

93

Chapter 5

What You Should Know

About MIDI

In MIDI, each note is stored as a list of attributes (just like images in vector graphics). Some common **attributes** of notes stored as MIDI data are:

- the type of **instrument**, e.g. violin, saxophone
- the **pitch** of the note, i.e. the frequency of the sound
- the **volume** of the note
- the **duration** of the note, i.e. how many seconds the note carries on for
- the **tempo**, i.e. how fast the notes are played.

Figure 5.14

Figure 5.15

These attributes describe all that is needed to play any tune on any instrument. The MIDI interface allows the creation and editing of tunes. Any note can be altered to achieve what the user requires.

MIDI keyboards, or other instruments, are used to create sound data in MIDI format. You don't even need the instruments, as there are software packages that allow you to create and edit MIDI files directly from your computer.

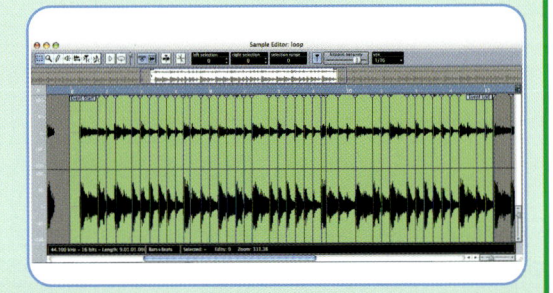

Figure 5.16

Chapter 5

Video data

Video data is a sequence of pictures, called **frames**, which are shown in sequence to simulate a moving image by tricking the brain into filling in the gaps. Just imagine one of those flip books where each page contains a small picture that is very slightly different from the one before it. You then quickly flick through the pages and the characters appear to move. Each of the pictures in a video clip is a **bitmap** image.

Hardware required

The basic hardware required to capture digital video is a digital video camera, or a webcam if the quality is less important. Each of these uses a bank of light sensors to capture the image, in the same way that a scanner does.

You would also need a graphics card, or video card, installed in your computer. This card is involved in the inputting and outputting of data to and from your computer. It may also do some processing if compression is involved.

Figure 5.17 A webcam

Key Points

Factors affecting file size and quality

A general rule is that anything that improves the quality will take more file space. The factors affecting the file size of a video clip are:

The **length** of the clip in seconds.

The number of **frames per second (fps)**, also called the *frame rate*, is very important in terms of both quality and file size. If the frame rate is set too low the action appears jerky; if it is too high then the amount of data to be stored is very large and the processor and/or graphics card will have to do a lot more work. Professional video is captured at 25 fps, cinema is 24 fps, and web cams are usually set at around 8 or 16 fps.

The number of colours available affects the size of each frame. The technical term is the **colour depth**, or often the *bit depth*. This is the same as for bitmapped images, with a number of bits or bytes needed to store each pixel. A typical range would be 8 bit colour, giving 256 possible colours, up to 32 bit colour with four billion colours.

The **resolution** of the image, measured in dots per inch (dpi), also affects the size of each frame and therefore the size of the clip. If the resolution is too low the video will be grainy. If it is set higher, the clip will be of high quality but will be very large. The resolution is often given as the screen dimensions in pixels, i.e. standard PAL video resolution is 768 × 576; this sum gives the number of pixels per frame.

MULTIMEDIA TECHNOLOGY

Chapter 5

Calculating the file size

The file size of a video clip is calculated by first finding the size of a single frame, using the resolution and colour depth. This is then multiplied by the frame rate and the number of seconds in the clip to get the final size. This is then reduced, by successive division, to obtain the file size in appropriate units (from bytes up to gigabytes).

Reducing file size by using compression

The file size can be reduced by using compression, which uses a sort of code to cut down on the data held. There are two basic types of file compression, **lossy compression** and **lossless compression**. The Intermediate 2 course concentrates on the first of these.

Key Points

Lossy compression

Lossy compression removes some of the data, keeping only what is necessary to convey the message. A crude example of text-based lossy compression is the removal of vowels from a sentence so that fewer letters need to be stored. What do these sentences say?

- 'F y cn rd ths sntnc thn w dd nt nd th vwls'
- 'Intrmdt tw Cmptng s nt t bd f y stdy'
- 'Cmprssn wrks, bt mstks cn hppn'

Lossy compression is applied to sound (MP3), video (MPEG) or bitmaps (JPEG). In each of these some quality is sacrificed to reduce file size.

Key Points

Lossless compression

The other alternative is lossless compression, which puts the message into a code so that **no data is lost** and the original message can be rebuilt.

Example

Using text as an example, the following code has been applied to a piece of text:

Text	' the '	'is '	'ed'	' and '	'or'	't '	' t'	' he '
Code	1	2	3	4	5	6	7	8

The passage below is to be compressed:

'Albert limped his way through the crowd. He was unhappy about the rain and wanted to get home before his dinner got cold. He usually liked Wednesdays as he got porridge in the morning.'

(184 characters)

Key Points continued ➢

Key Points continued

The passage now reads:

```
"Alber6limp3 h2way7hrough1crowd.8was unhappy
about1rain4want37o ge6home bef5e h2dinner go6cold.8usually
lik3 W3nesdays as8go6p5ridge in1m5ning."
```
(142 characters)

Lossless compression does need to be coded and decoded to be used/stored so there is a processing overhead to be taken into account.

What You Should Know

About file formats for video data

Video data is stored in either an uncompressed format, like the Windows-based Audio Video Interleave format (**AVI**), or one of many compressed formats.

One compressed format in common usage is **MPEG** (Motion Picture Experts Group). This format uses lossy compression to reduce file size. The technique involves storing only some of the frames in the clip. These **keys frames** are stored normally. The format then stores the differences between the individual frames. Storing the changes takes up less space than storing whole frames. Each key frame is stored as a JPEG graphic.

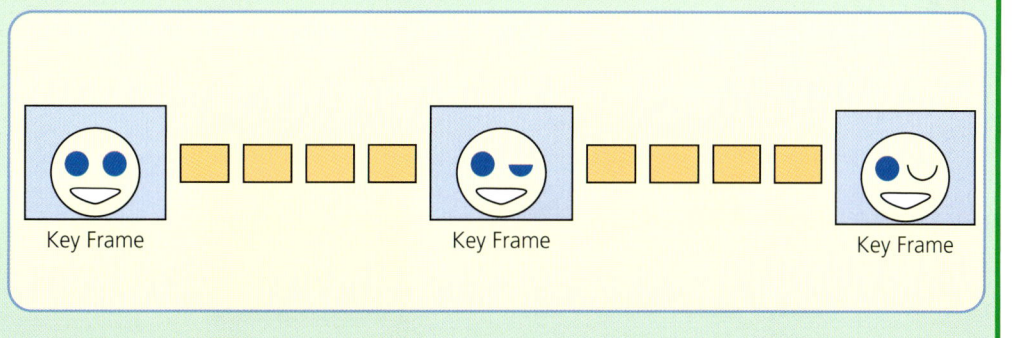

Key Frame — Key Frame — Key Frame

Figure 5.18 Lossy compression of video data

Chapter 5

Video editing software

In order to make anything of the clips that you have captured, whether from the Internet or using your digital video camera, you will need to edit them. The software you need might be bundled with your computer, as e.g. Windows MovieMaker, or you might buy a more fully-featured video editing suite, like Director.

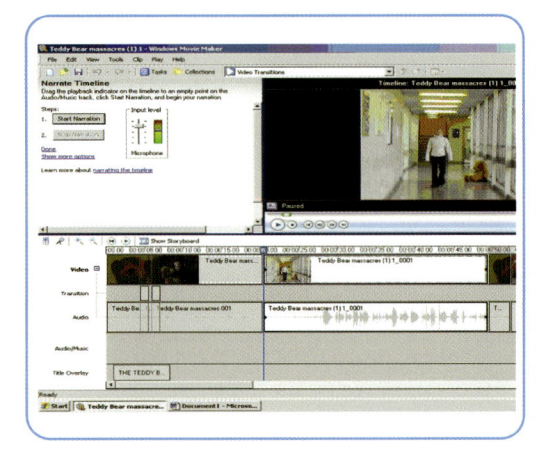

Figure 5.19 Windows MovieMaker

Key Points

Video editing software

The main features of simple video editing software are:
- The ability to **trim**, or **crop**, part of the video.
- The ability to **import** clips into your film or to **export** clips for use elsewhere.
- The ability to rearrange the sequence of clips according to a chosen **timeline**.
- The ability to add **transitions** like jump, fade or dissolve.
- The ability to add a **sound track**.
- The ability to add visual or sound **effects**.

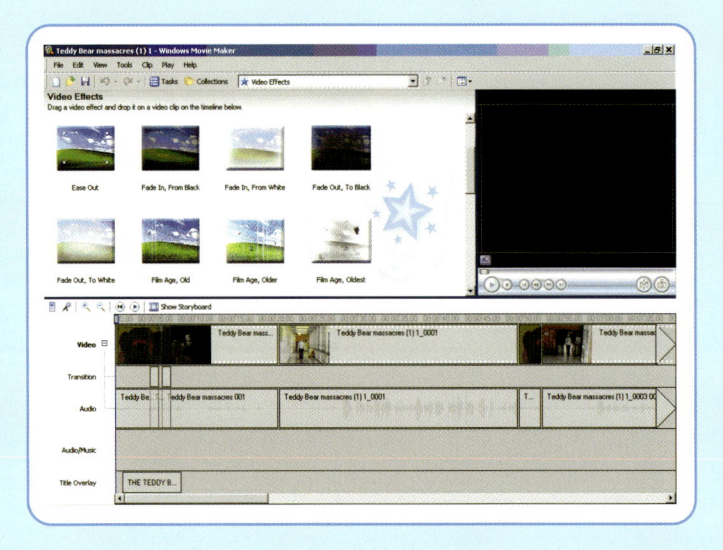

Figure 5.20 Video effects available with Windows MovieMaker

Chapter 5

MULTIMEDIA TECHNOLOGY

Vector graphics data

Vector graphics are another way of representing graphical data. A picture in a bitmapped graphic is made up of small squares of colour (pixels). In a vector, or object-oriented, graphic the image is made up of a number of shapes layered on top of one another to make up the picture.

Each object in the picture is described mathematically as a list of **attributes**. These fully describe the type of object, its **position** on screen, its **size** and the **colour/pattern** of its outline (called **line**) and middle (called **fill**). Other attributes might be the degree of any **rotation** and which **layer** it is on.

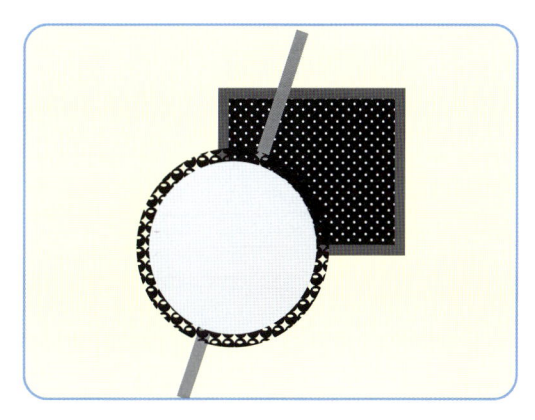

Figure 5.21

A typical object might be described in a vector graphics package as:

```
line(layer, startX, startY, endX, endY, line colour, line thickness, line pattern)
```

As more objects are added to the picture the file gets longer. This file is then read by the package and the objects are drawn on screen layer by layer. This means that the file size increases with the **complexity** of the image.

It is possible to draw three-dimensional (3-D) objects using vector graphics. All the package has to be able to do is to recognise the type of object and to interpret the list of attributes correctly. The attributes are the same as for flat (2-D) shapes, but with a few extra ones. Common 3-D attributes that are added are **angle of rotation**, **surface texture** and **shadow**.

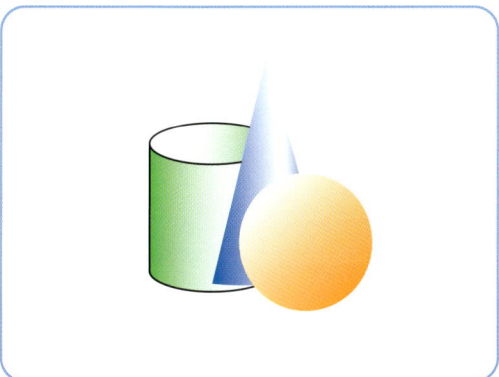

Figure 5.22

Advantages of vector graphics

There are several advantages of vector graphics over bitmaps:
- ◆ As they are a mathematical description of the shape, they can be redrawn to any scale without loss of quality. If you scale a bitmap it often becomes blocky. This ability to rescale without loss of quality is called **resolution independence**.
- ◆ Each object in the image is editable and can be duplicated, moved or manipulated easily.

99

Chapter 5

- Objects can be grouped together so that they are treated as a single unit.
- As each object is on its own layer, objects can be overlapped without destroying the object underneath.
- Simple vector graphics are much smaller, in terms of file size, than bitmaps, which store every pixel in the image.

Key Points

Common file types for vector graphics

There are few standard file types used to store graphics in vector formats, as each package tends to store the images in their own format. However, there are a few industry standards, particularly:

- SVG (scalable vector graphics)
- VRML (virtual reality modelling language)
- WRL (world description language).

Each of these allows a 3-D world to be defined as a group of objects, each described mathematically. All the advantages of vector graphics apply here, plus the ability to do 3-D modelling.

VRML (pronounced 'vermal') is used widely in smartphones and the web. You may find many sites still referring to it by the older name of 'virtual reality mark-up language'.

Questions

Q16 Name two items of hardware required to capture sound data.

Q17 Describe one way, other than compression, in which simple sound editing software could be used to decrease the file size of an audio clip.

Q18 What is meant by the term 'frame rate' (fps)?

Q19 State two common attributes of vector graphic objects.

Q20 Describe virtual reality modelling language (VRML) and give an example of its use.

Q21 Describe three common attributes of notes stored as MIDI data.

Chapter 6

FOCUS ON THE EXTERNAL EXAMINATION

The importance of your practical work

Your Standard Grade exam is worth 30% of your overall grade. The other 70% comes from the practical work you have done in class and will be completed well before you sit the exam. Make sure you work very hard at your practical tasks as they do count towards your final grade. Your teacher will tell you what your practical grade is.

Know your topics, solve your problems

In the written exam there will be questions which check your knowledge and understanding of the topics in the course. There will also be questions on problem-solving.

At the end of the course you will sit an exam.

Exam details

The Intermediate 2 exam has three sections together worth 70 marks. The exam lasts 1 hour and 30 minutes.

Section I is compulsory and consists of short-answer questions on Computer Systems and Software Development which are worth 15 marks altogether.

Section II is also compulsory and has questions that need fuller answers than those in Section I. This section is worth 30 marks altogether.

Section III has questions on your optional unit, either Networks, Artificial Intelligence or Multimedia Technology, and these are worth 25 marks altogether.

Exam preparation tips

- Draw up a revision plan well before the exam scheduling your revision so that you can cover it all without leaving it to the last minute.
- Use a checklist to make sure you cover all the topics.
- Learn the definitions of all the topics in the book.
- Check your knowledge is up to exam standard by answering all the questions in the book.
- Answer the following practice exam style questions, then check the answers.

Practice exam questions

The following questions are examples of the kind you will find in each section of your final Intermediate 2 exam paper.

Section I

1. What is the largest number that can be stored using 8 bits? — 2
2. Describe the function of a server on a client/server network. — 1
3. Describe one *function* an interface carries out when connected to a peripheral. — 1
4. What is a browser? — 1
5. A processor has registers. Name two other parts of a processor. — 2
6. How many megabytes are in 1.4 terabytes? — 1
7. Which Act is designed to make spreading computer viruses illegal? — 1

Section II

8. A small business purchases a new computer system for its LAN. The computer has a 2.4 Gigahertz processor and comes with a 17 inch TFT screen.

    (a) What does clock speed tell you about the performance of a system? — 1

    (b) Compare an LCD with a TFT monitor using two suitable characteristics. — 2

    (c) Name one input device that would be suitable for a laptop other than a keyboard. — 1

    Before the computer is fitted to the network anti-virus software is installed to prevent viruses spreading.

    (d) Describe two ways in which a virus might be spread. — 2

    (e) A business wants to send a letter to lots of customers at the same time. What feature of their email software could be used to do this? — 1

    (f) The letter which is being sent is saved using a standard file format. What advantage is there in using a standard file format? — 2

    (g) Describe two ways in which a WAN differs from a LAN. — 2

    (11)

9. Alex is writing a program that will add up marks in the Intermediate 2 Computing exam. There are seven questions, each of 10 marks.

    It will then display the total. The numbers are typed in by the user and must be in the range 1–10. The pseudocode for the design of the program is as follows:

    ```
    1. display instructions for user
    2. input and total 7 marks
    3. display total
    ```

    Refinement of step 2

```
2.1 set total to zero
2.2 loop 7 times
2.3 get mark from user
2.4 add mark to total
2.5 end loop
```

(a) State the name of the type of loop used in the refinement of step 2.   *1*

(b) Which of these standard algorithms is used in the refinement of step 2.3?
- Count occurrences
- Input validation
- Find maximum
- Linear search   *1*

(c) A set of test data used for the program included the following marks:

2, 4, 7, -1, 0, 10, 13

Explain why this is a good set of data to use to test the program fully.
Your answer should refer to the three types of test data.   *3*

(d) The values are to be held as a list. State a type of data structure that would be suitable to hold this data.   *1*

(e) Alex uses a compiler to convert the high level language into machine code.

    (i) State two reasons why Alex writes the program in a high level language rather than using machine code.   *2*

    (ii) Describe how the compiler translates the high level language into machine code.   *2*

(f) The final program will display the grade gained in an Intermediate 2 Computing exam using a conditional statement to display 'B' if the percentage is between 60 and 69 inclusive. The pseudocode for the conditional statement is shown below:

```
IF mark >= 60 OR mark <= 69 THEN display "B"
```

However, during testing it is discovered that "B" is displayed when the mark 25 is entered. Explain the error in the pseudocode.   *2*

(12)

Section III

Computer Networking

10. Jack runs a small business and is setting up a local area network at home which will be linked to the Internet.

(a) Jack decides to link the systems on his home network using a combination of cable and wireless connections. Describe one advantage of cable and one advantage of wireless connection.   *2*

(b) Jack's wife has a laptop which she wants to connect to the home LAN. What does she need to be fitted to her laptop before she can make any network connection?   *1*

(c) Before anyone on the home network can access the Internet, Jack has to sign up with an ISP. Describe one service an ISP provides.   *1*

(d) To protect his network Jack installs anti-virus software. Describe two other measures he can take to protect the data on his network.   *2*

(e) Jack enters the following URL into his web browser:

    http://www.grovel.co.uk

What does the .co.uk part of the URL tell you?   *1*

(f) When travelling, Jack's wife accesses the Internet using a web-enabled phone. This has a microbrowser.

Describe two differences between a microbrowser and a browser used on a desktop computer.   *2*

(g) Jack uses the Internet to buy and sell products for his company. Describe one advantage for his business of using the Internet.   *1*

    (10)

Artificial Intelligence

11. QwikFIX is a company giving advice on setting up computer networks in small businesses. It has asked a software company to write an *expert system* to help configure these networks and to help identify and solve problems.

(a) Suggest two reasons why QwikFIX believes it needs an 'expert system', rather than relying on human experts.   *2*

(b) Suggest one reason why customers may have concerns over the possible use of the 'expert system'.   *2*

(c) What is the name given to the list of facts and rules in the expert system?   *1*

(d) The software company is concerned that the customers of QwikFIX may try to sue them if their networks do not work properly.

Describe a precaution they can take to prevent them being sued by the customers.   *1*

(e) Expert systems were first developed in the 1970s. Modern expert systems use many more facts and rules.

Explain one hardware development that has made this possible.   *2*

    (8)

12. A knowledge base has been created to hold information on house sales of a group of estate agents. It contains facts about the agents and rules to decide if they should get a holiday bonus.

1   sales(amber,83).   % Amber has sold 83 houses this year
2   sales(bob,142).
3   sales(thomas,75).
4   sales(tanith,113).
5   sales(james,59).
6   female(tanith).   % Tanith is female
7   female(amber).
8   male(james).
9   male(bob).
10 male(thomas).
11 bonus(X) if sales(X, Y) and Y >100   % Give a bonus if X sells more than 100

(a) What would be the **first** result of the following query?

?male(X).   *1*

(b) What would be the result of the following query?

? bonus(james).   *1*

(c) What would be **all** the results of the following query?

? bonus(X).   *2*

(d) Use the line numbers to help you trace how the system evaluates the following query as far as the first solution.

? bonus(X).   *2*

(6)

Multimedia Technology

13. Morag is a music journalist writing for an online music magazine called 'Finding Emo'. The magazine publishes articles on its multimedia website.

(a) She is writing an article about a popular new band, 'Camouflage Hoodie', and she wants to include some high *resolution* photographs in her article.

  i) State **one** item of hardware that would allow her to capture photographs of the band in concert for the website.   *1*

  ii) Explain what is meant by the term **resolution**.   *1*

(b) Morag records some of the band's music. The audio software allows her to change the *sampling frequency*. She chooses the highest setting for recording each song.

  i) What effect will recording the sound at this setting have on the **size** of the sound file?   *1*

ii) What effect will recording the sound at this setting have on the sound **quality**?   *1*

(c) Morag wants to include **part** of a new unreleased song, 'Touch it and you're toast!', on the webpage.

    i) Name the feature of her sound editing software that will allow her to make this sound clip.   *1*

    ii) Name an **effect** that the sound editing software will allow her to add to the audio track.   *1*

(d) What item of hardware, other than speakers, is needed in a computer to output the sound from the website.   *1*

(e) The band has recorded a special message for their fans. This can be downloaded from the website as a *compressed* audio file.

    i) The file uses *lossy compression*. Describe **lossy** compression.   *1*

    ii) Name an audio file format that uses lossy compression.   *1*

    (9)

14. Iain is developing a multimedia tool for teaching trombone.

(a) He wants to include audio clips of tunes to practise.

Some of the audio is stored in MIDI format.

State **two** attributes of a note in MIDI.   *2*

(b) He is creating textured 3-D objects that can be rotated to show images of the musical instruments from different angles.

    i) Suggest a suitable 'texture' that can be applied to an object.   *1*

    ii) Name a format for storing 3-D objects in the application or on the Internet.   *1*

(c) Sections of video showing good technique are also to be included.

In the first version of the video the action appears jerky.

Describe **one** possible reason for this.   *1*

(d) Some of the photographs in the application are taken with a digital camera and others have been scanned.

    i) What **hardware** component is used in both digital cameras and scanners to capture the image.   *1*

    ii) Describe how increasing **resolution** of the photograph affects file size.   *1*

    (7)

ANSWERS

Chapter 1: Computer Systems

Q1 47 = 00101111, 80 = 01010000, 34 = 00100010

Q2 Floating point is easy to implement and saves storage space.

Q3 1222880 megabytes.

Q4 Text.

Q5 They represent control functions, not text.

Q6 = 4 × 5 × 600 × 600 = 7200000 bits = 900000 bytes = 879 Kbytes = .86 Mbytes.

Q7 It is the 'brains' of the computer that deals with all the movement of data and any calculations to be carried out.

Q8 It carries out all the computer's arithmetic and logical functions.

Q9 Registers are small temporary memory locations located on the processor.

Q10 Main memory is located inside the computer system. Backing storage = all storage devices outside of the main processor.

Q11 When the system is switched off data in RAM is lost and data in ROM is retained.

Q12 These are small-scale computer systems, complete with their own processors and memory, built into the machine to enable it to carry out its functions.

Q13 (a) A laptop is portable and can run on batteries.

    (b) A mainframe has much more powerful processors and very much larger backing storage capacity and main memory.

Q14 Gigahertz GHz.

Q15 Answers from the Internet.

Q16

Input a graphic from a book	Scanner
Control a pointer on a laptop	Touchpad
Capture and send pictures across the Internet	Web cam
Capture sound	Microphone

Q17 Any two of: resolution, cost, capacity.

Q18 Answers from the Internet.

Q19 Answers from the Internet.

Q20 CD-ROM capacity = 700 megabytes, single-sided DVD capacity = 4.7 gigabytes.

Q21 Portable backing storage.

Q22 Tape.

Q23 (a) To connect peripherals to the computer system.

(b) Any two of: change electrical voltages; deal with control signals; change analogue data to digital form; store incoming data so that the processor can get on with other tasks.

Q24

Telecommunications are used on a:	WAN
The media used on a LAN are:	copper cable, fibre-optic cable, co-axial cable or short range wireless
The maximum spread of a LAN is:	Two kilometres
The bandwidth on a LAN using copper cable can be:	100 Mbits per second

Q25 Any two of: share peripherals such as hard drives and printers; share data and programs; work on shared projects; communicate by sending emails; backup data more effectively; control security more effectively.

Q26 (a) A mailing list contains all the email addresses of the people in a group.

(b) A browser is a program that helps you navigate the world wide web, move between and look at web pages.

(c) Hyperlinks are used to link web pages together.

(d) Search engines are used to find web pages.

Q27 Low cost of telecoms services, ability to share expensive equipment; networks let businesses and families keep in touch around the world; need for instant access to information.

Q28 Individuals to whom data relates are known as data subjects.

The data controller is the person, business or organisation that controls the collection and use of personal data.

A data user is an individual within an organisation who makes use of personal data.

Q29 Any three from the list on page 23.

Q30 Interfering with a system so that it doesn't run properly, making changes to the system to prevent others accessing the system, making changes to the software or data.

Q31 Any three from the list on page 24.

Q32 Any three from: it runs other software, controls peripherals, monitors the operation of the computer, provides the HCI for the user.

Q33 Without the OS no other tasks could take place.

Q34 Any three from: spreadsheet, word processor, database, graphics.

Q35 Files can be read by a wide range of applications.

Q36 An RTF would have all the formatting included in the file, e.g. indents, spacing, text styles, margin settings, etc.

Q37 Viruses attach themselves to applications, games, system files and even data files such as word processing documents or graphics.

Q38 People swapping or lending CDs, email attachments. Viruses can use your email address book to spread themselves.

Chapter 2: Software Development

Q1 Implementation and documentation.

Q2 Analysis specifies exactly what problem is to be solved. Maintenance is where changes are made to the program after it has been delivered to the client.

Q3 Pseudocode allows a solution to the problem to be designed in an English-like language which is easy to translate into a high level language.

Q4 Flow charts show the flow of control within a program. Structure charts show how code blocks relate to each other and can include information on data flow.

Q5 Normal (23, 50 or any in range data), extreme (0, 100, the boundaries) and exceptional (–1, 101, 23.4, 'albert' or any data outside the range).

Q6 An interpreter translates and executes each line in turn. A compiler translates each line in the program and then runs the translated version of the whole program.

Q7 HLL use variables, subroutines, control structures (like conditional loops).

Q8 A text editor is used for entering or editing code.

Q9 (num >= 18 AND num <= 30).

Q10 A loop which is inside another loop.

Q11 Any array of strings.

Q12 Linear Search.

Q13 INT, ROUND, LEN, UCASE$.

Q14 Predefined functions do not have to be designed, they have been coded, they have been tested and they have been documented.

Q15 Find Minimum (Note: the shortest time is the fastest).

Q16 The software matches the software specification from the analysis phase. It does all the tasks it is supposed to do.

Q17 Readability makes the purpose of software sections clear. Enables tester/programmer to find relevant code sections during debugging/testing process.

Q18 Meaningful variable names, comment lines, subroutines/modules, effective use of white space (indentation and/or blanks lines).

Q19 User guide and technical guide.

Chapter 3: Computer Networking

Q1 A browser.

Q2 The first part 'http' is the protocol. The second part 'www.visit-fortwilliam' indicates which server the web page is stored on. The third part 'co.uk' indicates the type of organisation that is storing the web pages.

Q3 Back and forward buttons, history, favourites.

Q4 Microbrowsers are browsers that allow mobile phones to send and receive email and browse the web.

Q5 The interactivity and full multimedia features of web pages are unavailable in microbrowsers.

Q6 Any two advantages and disadvantages from the list on page 50.

Q7 Any three of: works with your browser to fetch web pages; provides web-based email and messaging services; gives access to newsgroups and chat rooms; gives users space to store their own web pages.

Q8 (a) Orders can be taken and dealt with instantly; people can work from home saving on the time and cost of travelling to work.

(b) Lower costs: there is no need for shops or people to work in them; advertising costs are also reduced; orders can be taken and dealt with instantly.

Q9 Different computer technologies are coming together with products we use in our everyday lives e.g. phones that can access the Internet, TVs that can access the Internet and send email.

Q10 (a) Students have access to a wealth of network-based information. Staff can use the network to communicate with students and other staff.

(b) Any two from the list on page 53.

Q11 Any two from the list on page 53.

Q12 Guidelines to make sure that people's use of the network stays within the laws and guidelines about how to respect other people and their rights when using the network.

Q13 Physical: locks on doors, locks on workstations, no removeable storage devices.
Software: IDs, passwords, encryption, biometric systems.

Q14 When networks can't send data because cables are damaged or wireless signals suffer from interference.

Q15

Topic	Description	Why it is needed
Internet content filtering	Checks the content of web pages and blocks those that are not suitable.	Unsuitable web pages on the Internet.
Backup strategy	Keeping multiple copies of important data.	In case data is lost.
Encryption	Encoding data.	In case security is breached by a hacker.

Q16 Answers must contain at least one point from each list on page 56.

Q17

A WPAN is	A wireless personal area network.
A WLAN is	A wireless local area network.
A WWAN is	A wireless wide area network.

Q18 A cable modem connection uses cable television network instead of telephone lines to send data, and a broadband ADSL connection uses telephone lines to send data at high speeds.

Q19

A domain name is	an organisation's unique name on the Internet.
The domain name system is	used to change the domain name into its associated address which is then used to find that organisation on the Internet.
Host name resolution is	the process of changing the domain name into an Internet address.

Chapter 4: Artificial Intelligence

Q1 Any two from: learning, language, creativity, problem-solving.

Q2 Human tester sits at two terminals. One terminal is linked to a human, the other to the system being tested for AI. The tester 'converses' with two subjects using each terminal. If tester cannot tell the difference, the system has AI.

Q3 Domain expert provides expert knowledge (facts and rules). Knowledge engineer programs these facts and rules into the expert system.

Q4 Eliza, Parry, SHRDLU.

Q5 Any two from: ease of distribution/multiple copies; available 24 hours a day; knowledge not lost if expert moves/dies; consistency of advice.

Q6 One from: postcode recognition using best-fit to templates; stock market forecasts based upon past performances; weather prediction using satellite photos and historical records.

Q7 Any two from: distinguish between shadows and edges; depth perception; recognise unfamiliar objects; real-time processing to avoid collisions.

Q8 Voice recognition/NLP – will interpret user commands to call numbers.

Q9 Able to react to surroundings; able to make decisions; able to function if it loses contact with base.

Q10 Uses NLP to recognise phonemes, combines these to produce words, interprets meaning, selects/generates appropriate response.

Q11 Indistinct voices (accent/illness), ambiguity of words (e.g. soldiers charged); similar sounding words (would/wood, witch/which).

Q12 Jonny writes out a set of training phrases designed to cover all basic letter shapes and combinations. System learns his handwriting.

Q13 Goal is the knowledge we are looking for; subgoals are what need to be true to reach that goal; and trace is the method of describing the path taken through the knowledge base in order to arrive at the goal.

Q14 Any two from: sound sensor for detecting noise, movement sensor to detect movement, heat sensor to follow residual heat patterns.

Q15 Any two from: faster processors, larger memory, larger storage capacity.

Q16 One from: noughts and crosses, chess, draughts.

Q17 Breadth-first: ABCDEFG, Depth-first: ABDECFG.

Q18
```
has(mammal,lactation).
has(mammal,warm_blood).
has(mammal,live_birth).
has(vertebrate,backbone).
has(bat,wings).
is_a(mammal,vertebrate).
is_a(bat,mammal).
is_a(dog,mammal).
has(dog,waggly_tail).
is_a(spaniel,dog).
is_a(great_dane,dog).
is_a(jill,great_dane).
is_a(horseshoe,bat).
is_a(long_eared,bat).
is_a(pipistrelle,bat).
```

Chapter 5: Multimedia Technology

Q1 Analysis, design, implementation, testing, documentation, evaluation and maintenance.

Q2 A browser or a viewer (player).

Q3 Digital cameras use electronic circuits called charged coupled devices, CCD, to capture light coming in through a lens.

Q4 Reduces it.

Q5 Compressing a graphic file size without losing any data e.g. GIF file format.

Q6 Compressing a graphic file size by losing data e.g. JPEG file format.

Q7 256.

Q8 Trebles the file size and improves the quality of the graphic.

Q9 Improves the quality and increases the file size.

Q10 Lets you cut out the parts of the graphic you don't want.

Q11 Distortion, 3-D, textures.

Q12 TFT is more expensive but produces higher quality displays than an LCD.

Q13 So that it can relieve the main processor of the pressure of processing and storing the graphics.

Q14 It combines phone technology with the mobile computing technology that you would find on a palmtop and digital camera technology.

Q15 Because the user is immersed in the world of the computer and can journey through, and interact with, a computer generated 3-D multimedia world.

Q16 A microphone and a sound card are required to capture sound data.

Q17 Reducing the sampling frequency or sample depth would lower file size.

Q18 Frame rate (fps) is the number of frames per second (25 fps is standard video rate).

Q19 Any two from: line thickness; line colour; line pattern; fill colour; fill pattern; co-ordinates.

Q20 VRML is used to describe 3-D objects in web pages. It can be used to define virtual worlds in the Internet.

Q21 Any three from: instrument, pitch, volume, duration and tempo are common attributes of MIDI data.

Chapter 6: Practice exam questions

Section I

1. 255. *2*

2. A server provides resources for clients on a network e.g. file server. *1*

3. One of: change electrical voltages, deal with control signals; change analogue data to digital form; store incoming data so that the processor can get on with other tasks. 1

4. A browser is a program that helps you navigate the world wide web, move between and look at web pages. 1

5. ALU, CU. 2

6. =1.4 *1024 = 1433.6 1

7. Computer Misuse Act. 1

Section II

8. (a) The clock speed gives some indication of the performance of a processor but it is not the only factor determining how well a processor performs. 1

   (b) Resolution: A TFT screen will produce a much higher quality display than an LCD. It will also cost more than an LCD. 2

   (c) Touchpad. 1

   (d) People swapping or lending CDs; email attachments. 2

   (e) Mailing lists. 1

   (f) Your data files are very portable and can be transferred easily from one package to another. 2

   (g) Geographical spread: a WAN spans a much larger area. 2

   Transmission media: a LAN will use cables or short distance wireless transmission, a LAN will use telecommincation links including phone networks and satellites.

9. (a) Fixed loop (will also accept FOR…NEXT loop). 1

   (b) Input validation. 1

   (c) It contains in range (2, 4 and 7), out of range (-1 and 13) and boundary data (0 and 10). (These categories are also called normal, exceptional and extreme.) 3

   (d) Array (of integers). 1

   (e) (i) Easier to spot mistakes, easier to understand, easier to learn. 2

   (ii) Compiler translates program line by line, translated program is then executed. 2

   (f) The OR should be an AND. Every number is accepted if an OR is used. 2

Section III

10. (a) Cable will give a reliable high speed connection e.g. 100 Mbps. 2

    Wireless gives you mobility since it avoids the need for cabling.

    (b) An interface. 1

	(c)	Any one of: works with your browser to fetch web pages; provides web-based email and messaging services; gives access to newsgroups and chat rooms; gives users space to store their own web pages.	1
	(d)	Use encryption and passwords.	2
	(e)	That it is a business company based in the UK.	1
	(f)	Microbrowsers don't have all the features of a browser for a desktop/laptop and they lack its interactivity.	2
	(g)	One of: lower costs; ability to reach a worldwide market; speed of transactions.	1
11.	(a)	Consistency of advice; 24-hour availability of advice; comparatively cheap; human experts can leave the company; system can be duplicated many times.	2
	(b)	May not trust advice of machine, humans are more flexible, humans can use common sense, user of expert system may need special training.	2
	(c)	Knowledge base.	1
	(d)	Company can include a disclaimer that states that the system is used at the risk of the client.	1
	(e)	More powerful processors mean that facts and rules can be checked faster and a solution found in a shorter time. Cheaper/faster memory means that larger knowledge bases can be held and manipulated. Each of these mean that more complex problems can be solved in a reasonable time.	2
12.	(a)	X = james	1
	(b)	no (accept false)	1
	(c)	X = bob, X = tanith	2
	(d)	The full trace would look something like this…	

- Goal is bonus(X)
- Match at line 11, first subgoal is sales(X, Y)
- Match at line 1, X=amber, Y=83
- Second subgoal 83 > 100 fails 1
- Match first subgoal at line 2, X = bob, Y = 142
- Second subgoal 142 > 100 succeeds.
- Goal succeeds. Return X = bob 1

13.	(a)	i) Digital camera (scanner is not a good answer here).	1
		ii) Resolution is the number of pixels in a given area (measured in dots per inch)	
		NOTE: 'number of pixels in the image' is not correct as the image may be huge.	1

	(b)	i)	The file size will be increased.	1
		ii)	The quality will be improved.	1
	(c)	i)	Cropping.	1
		ii)	Echo, increase volume, reverse, reverb…	1
	(d)		Sound card.	1
	(e)	i)	Lossy compression cuts out part of the audio data with minimal effect on the quality.	1
		ii)	MP3 uses lossy compression. Also MP4, ADPCM and WMA.	1
14.	a)		Pitch, volume, tempo…	2
	(b)	i)	Shadow, surface texture, reflection.	1
		ii)	VRML.	1
	(c)		Frame rate too low, wrong software.	1
	(d)	i)	Charged Coupled Device (CCD).	1
		ii)	Increased file size.	1

INDEX

A
access rights 54
addresses 20, 50
ADITDEM mnemonic 29
ADSL (broadband) 58
AI *see* artificial intelligence
algorithms 30, 31, 46–7
analysis stage, software
    development 29
AND operators 43–4
ANS *see* artificial neural systems
answers to questions 105–13
anti-virus software 27
application programs 25
arguments 63, 74–5
arithmetic and logic unit 6
arrays 41
artificial intelligence (AI) 60–79
   applications 64–70
   development 60–3
   exam questions 104
  knowledge representation 72–9
   search techniques 70–2
artificial neural systems (ANS) 65–6
ASCII code 3, 25
assignment 39–40
attachments 50–1
audio 88, 90, 91
AVI format 97

B
backing storage 7, 14–15
backup strategies 55
binary numbers 2
biometric systems 54
bitmap images 82, 95
black & white graphics 4
bomb-disposal robots 70
breadth-first searches 71–2
broadband (ADSL) connections 58
broadcast transmission 56
browsers 21
  see also microbrowsers; web
    browsers

C
cameras 82
CDs (compact disks) 15
character sets 3
chatterbots 63

clock speeds 9
codes 3, 25, 31–2
codes of conduct 53–4
colour 83, 95, 99
compact disks (CDs) 15
comparison operators 76–7
compilers 35–7
complex conditions 43–4
compression 82–3, 91, 96
Computer Misuse Act 24
computer systems 2–28
  backing storage devices 14–15
  data representation 2
  input devices 10–11
  law 22–5
  output devices 11–14
  software 25–7
  structure 5–7
  types 7–8
conditional loops 42–3
conditional statements 41–2
connections, Internet 57–9
content
  attachments 50
  filtering 55
control characters 4
copyright 24

D
data
  access types 16
  controllers 22, 23
  encryption 55
  representation 2
  subjects 22, 23
  transfer speed 11
  transmission 56
  types 39
  users 22, 23
Data Protection Act 22–5
databases 26
depth-first searches 71–2
design 29–31
desktop computers 8
dialup connections 57
digital cameras 10
digital television (DTV) 87
direct access 16
DNS (domain name system)
    58

documentation 33
domain names 58
DTV (digital television) 87
DVDs 16

E
E-commerce 52
editing
  audio 92
  images 84–5
  text 38
  video 98
Eliza program 62–3
email 19–20, 50
embedded systems 7
encryption 55
equipment sharing 21
evaluation 33–4
exams 101–4
expert systems 64–5

F
face recognition 67
favourites 48
File Transfer Protocol (ftp)
    49, 51
files
  formats 25, 97
  size 83, 91, 95, 96
  transfer 49, 50–1
  vector graphics 100
  video 95, 96, 97
filtering content 55
fitness for purpose 33
fixed loops 40
flash drives 16
floating point representation 2
floppy disks 14
folders 20
formats
  audio 90
  files 25, 97
  text 26
frames 95, 97
ftp (File Transfer Protocol) 49, 51
functions 45

G
game playing 60–1
goals 70, 73, 75

117

Index

graphics 26
   cards 86
   compression 82–3
   design notation 30
   display 85–6
   representation 2, 4
   see also vector graphics

H
handwriting recognition 68
hard disks 15
hardware
   AI 61
   graphics 85–6
   video 95
   wireless LANs 58
high level languages 35, 39–46
host name resolution 58
http (hypertext transfer protocol) 49
hyperlinks 20, 48

I
IDs (security) 54
IF statements 41–2
images 82, 84–5
   see also graphics
implementation 31–2
Information Commissioner 24
inkjet printers 13
input commands 39–46
input devices 10–11, 88
input validation 46–7
instantiation 75
intelligence 60
interfaces 17–18, 33
Internet 10, 20–1, 48–9, 53, 57–9
Internet Service Providers (ISPs) 51
internetworks 19
interpreters 35–7
ISDN connections 57
ISPs (Internet Service Providers) 51

J
JPEG 83
junk mail 50

K
keyboards 10
keys, software 55

knowledge (AI) 64, 72–9

L
languages 35–46, 62–3, 72–5
LANs see local area networks
laptop computers 8
laser printers 13
law 22–5
LCD see Liquid Crystal Display
leased line connections 57
Liquid Crystal Display (LCD) 12, 86
Lisp language 63
local area networks (LANs) 18
logic units 6
logical operators 43–4
loops 40, 42–3, 44–5
lossless compression 82–3, 96–7
lossy compression 91, 96
loudspeakers 13

M
machine code 35
macros 37–8
magnetic storage devices 14–15
mailing lists 20
mainframe computers 8
maintenance phase 34
memory 3, 7
mice 10
microbrowsers 49
microphones 10, 89
MIDI format 93–4
mobile phones 49
modem connections 57
monitors 11–12, 85–6
MP3 format 90
MPEG format 97
multicast 56
multimedia technology 80–100
   applications 80–4
   implementation 80, 81
   stages 80

N
natural language processing (NLP) 62–3
nested loops 44–5
networking/networks 18–19, 21, 48–59
   applications 48–54
   exam questions 103–4

growth 53
security 54–6
voice transmission 56
wireless communication 56–7
neural nets 65, 66
NLP see natural language processing
NOT operators 43–4
notation, graphics 30
number representation 2
numeric variables 39

O
objects 26
operating systems 25
operations 26
operators 43–4, 76–7
optical storage 15–16
OR operators 43–4
output commands 39–46
output devices 11–14

P
paint programs 84–5
palmtop computers 7–8
passwords 54
Patents Act 24
pattern recognition 66
performance measure 9
phones see mobile phones; smartphones
pocket PCs 87
pre-defined functions 45
predicate 74
presentation software 81
printers 13
processors 6
Prolog language 63
pseudocode 30, 31

Q
quality, file size 95

R
Random Access Memory (RAM) 7
random (direct) access 16
RAW format 90
re-writing disks 15
Read Only Memory (ROM) 7
readability 34
readable codes 31–2
reading email 19

Index

real numbers 2
registers 6, 24
replying to email 20
resolution 83, 95, 99
rich text format (RTF) 26
robots 69–70
ROM *see* Read Only Memory
rotation 99
RTF *see* rich text format
rules 61, 63, 75–6

S

sampling audio 91
scanners 10, 82
screens *see* monitors
search engines 21, 51
search techniques 70–2
security 54–6
semantic nets 72–3
sending email 20
sensors 69, 88
sequential data access 16
sharing equipment 21
size
   files 83, 91, 95, 96
   memory 3
smartphones 87
software 25–7
   keys 55
   languages 35–8
   security 54–5
   sound editing 92
software development 29–47
   analysis stage 29
   areas 29
   design 29–31
   documentation 33
   evaluation 33–4
   implementation 31–2
   languages 35–46
   maintenance phase 34

   process 29–34
   stages 29
   testing phase 33
solution tracing 77–8
sound
   cards 89, 90
   data 89–94
   editing software 92
   see also audio
sound time 91
speech recognition 68
speed, data transfer 11
spreadsheets 26
storage 4, 7, 82
string variables 39
structure, computer systems 5–7
synthesised sound data 93–4

T

tape 15
technology 52–3, 80–100
testing phase 33
text
   editors 38, 81
   formats 26
   representation 2
Thin Film Transistor (TFT) screens 12, 86
touchpads 10
trackpads 10
translators 35–7
transmission, data 56
trees (search) 70–1
true basic (language) 39–47
Turing test 60, 61

U

unicast 56
URLs (universal resource locators) 49

V

validation 46–7
variables 39, 74
vector graphics 99–100
video
   data 95–8
   editing software 98
   files 97
   output 88
video disks *see* DVDs
virtual reality 88–9
viruses 27, 50
vision systems 67–8
visual basic (language) 39–47
voice transmission 56

W

WANs *see* wide area networks
WAP *see* Wireless Application Protocol
WAV format 90
web browsers 48
web pages 20
webcams 10
wide area networks (WANs) 18
Wireless Application Protocol (WAP) 49
wireless communication 56–8
WLAN *see* wireless communication
word processors 26
world wide web (WWW) 20–1
   see also Internet
WPAN *see* wireless communication
writing disks 15
WWAN *see* wireless communication
WWW *see* world wide web
WYSIWYG 81